Table of Contents

Into Africa: Visiting Four National Parks in Tanzania

Like all great national parks you visit, there's the build up of the long drive. Our guide pointed to a herd of zebras off in the distance. We had just met our four travel mates, two American couples, well-suited for us on this adventure, and all were thrilled with our first sighting as we made our way south out of the city of Arusha toward the turn-off for Tarangire N.P. It is best known for its Baobab and Ebony trees, and elephants.

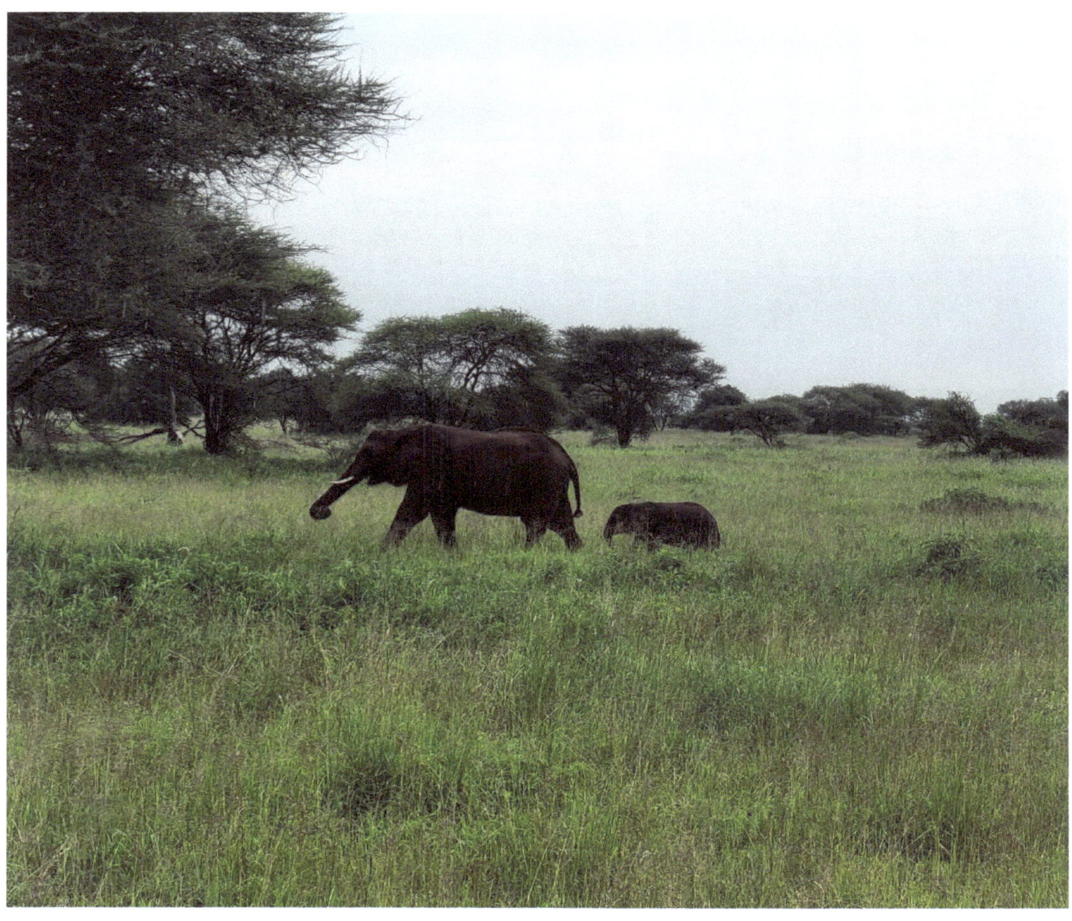

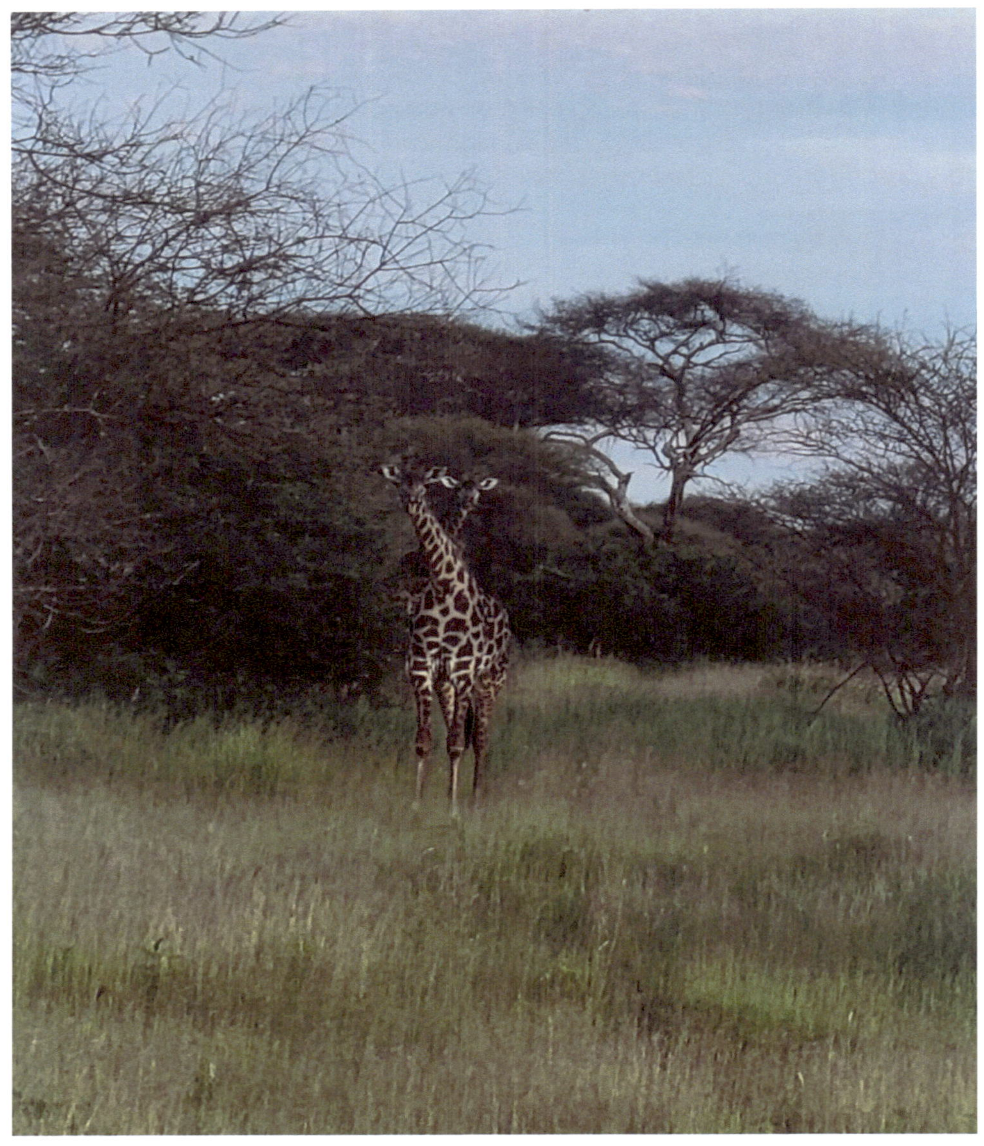

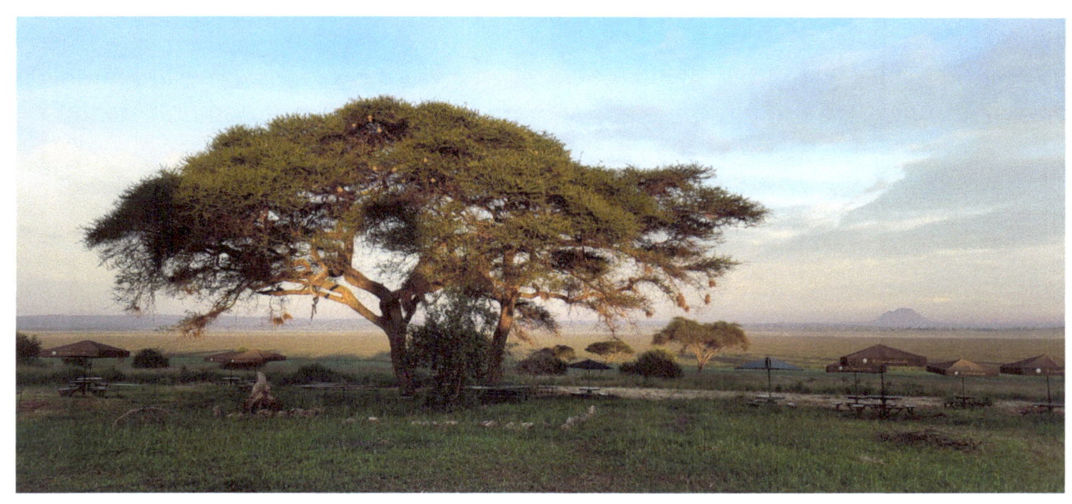

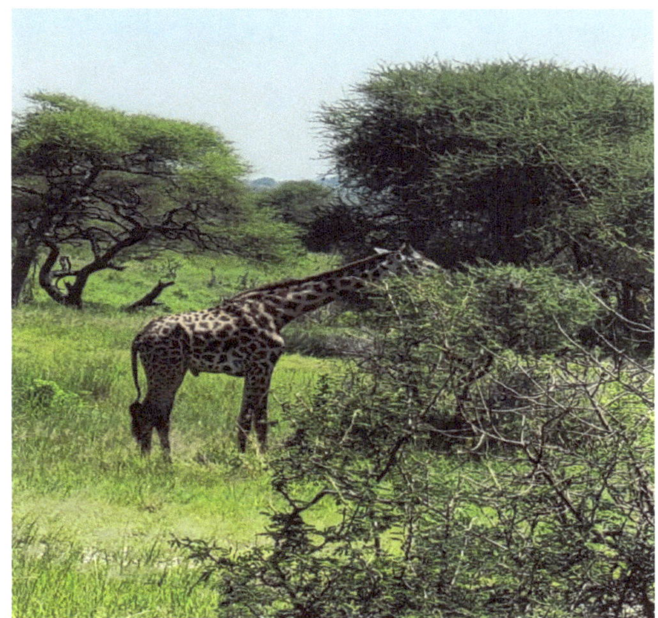

One thing you come across are the relic skulls of the old, or killed by predator, wild animals in Tanzania. Here, and on the next page, are the giraffe, elephant and buffalo, and a very much living Superb Starling.

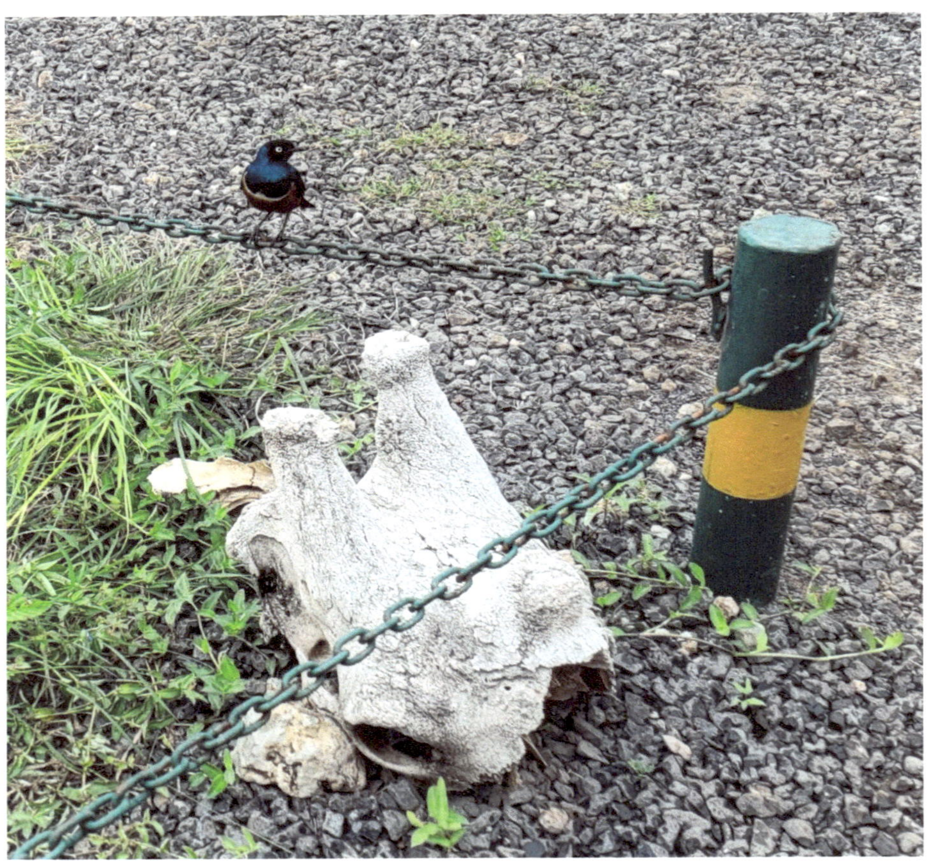

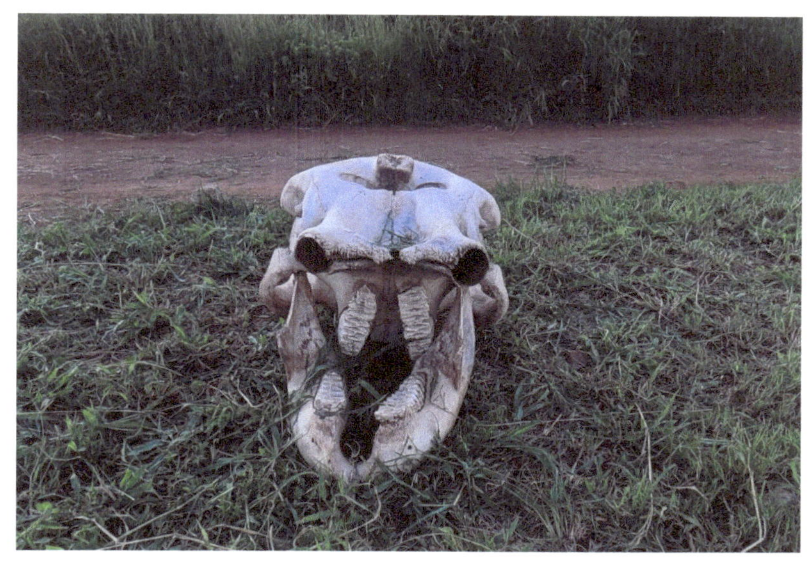

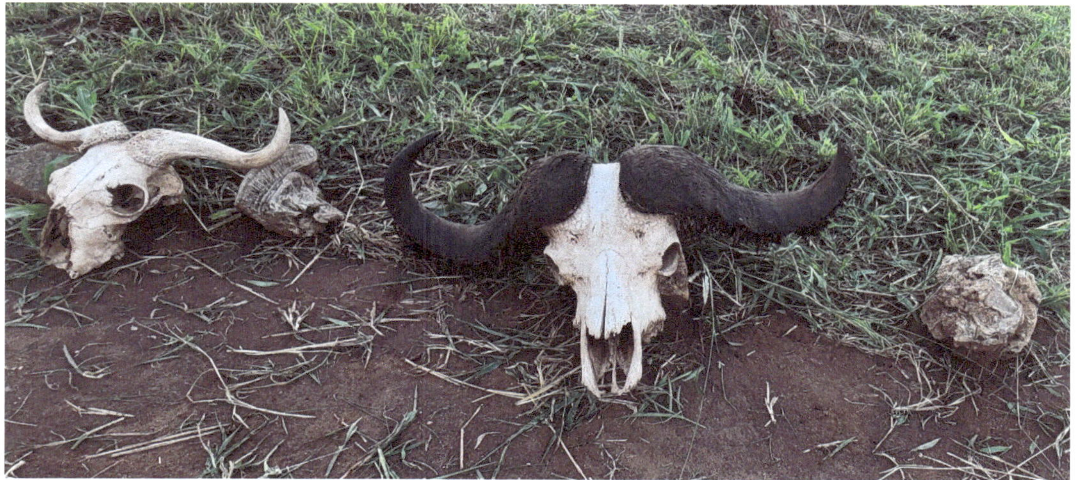

Tarangire National Park

Tarangire N. P., home of the Baobab (one very scary one), Elephants and Ebony Trees ... and huge termite mounds, and Tse-tse flies that prevented people from trying to settle there, and thereby enabled the formation of the park (the Tarangire species are harmless).

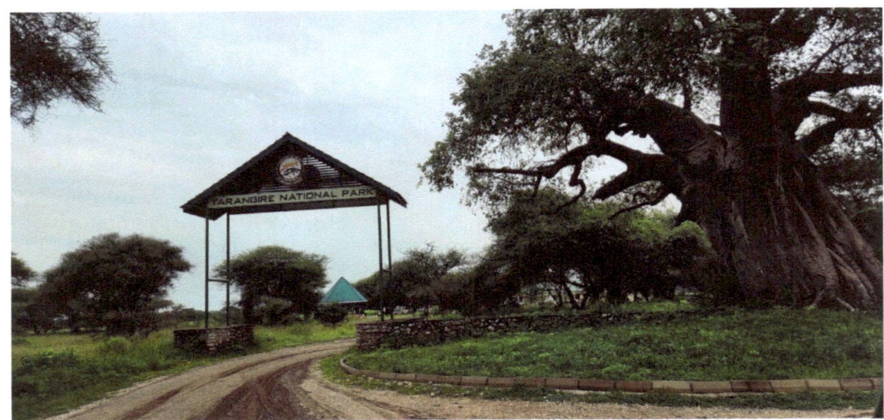

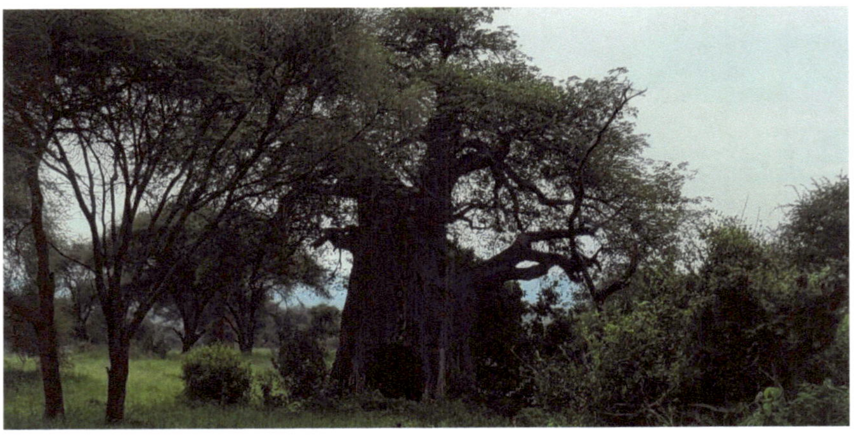

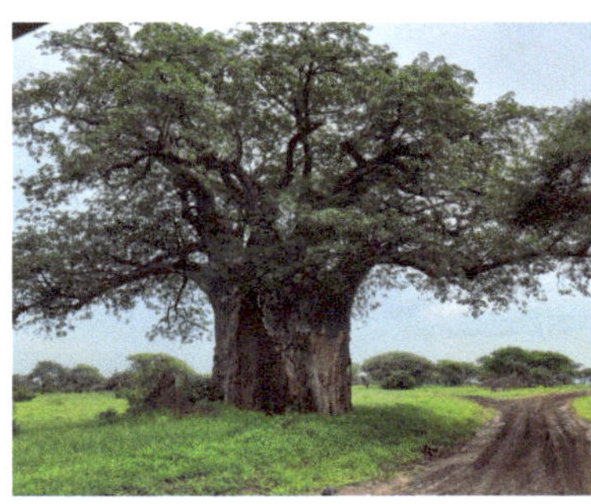 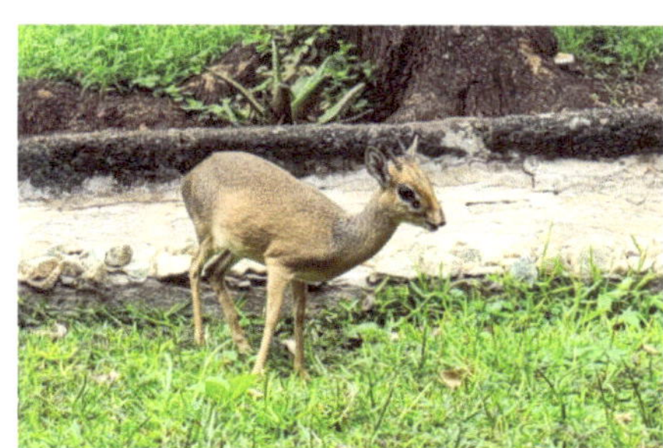 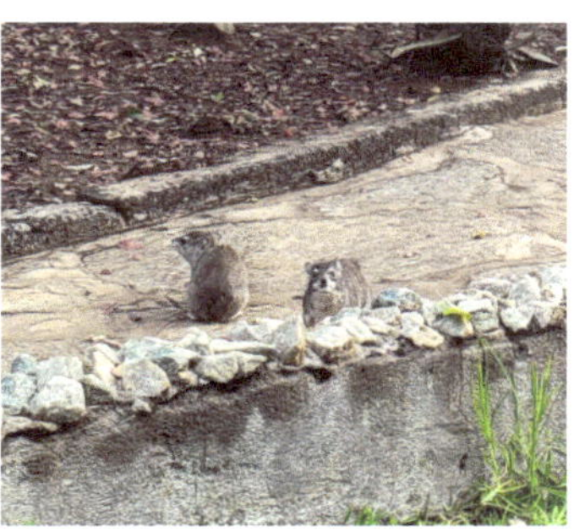

The Tarangire lodge where we stayed was visited regularly by the tiny Dik Dik Antelope and is home of rooftop-sunbathing Rock Hyrax (Gr: shrew-mouse), the lowly creature mentioned in the Bible. It's closest relative is the Elephant. And it can climb trees.

There is fine dining on the Tarangire N. P. savanna for Kori Bustards, lots of Spring insects to devour – the keystone Dung Beetle, grasshoppers, termites, bush crickets, and locusts and caterpillars when they're in season. There are nice clumps for cover, lots of space for the largest flying (heavy) bird in Africa to take off.

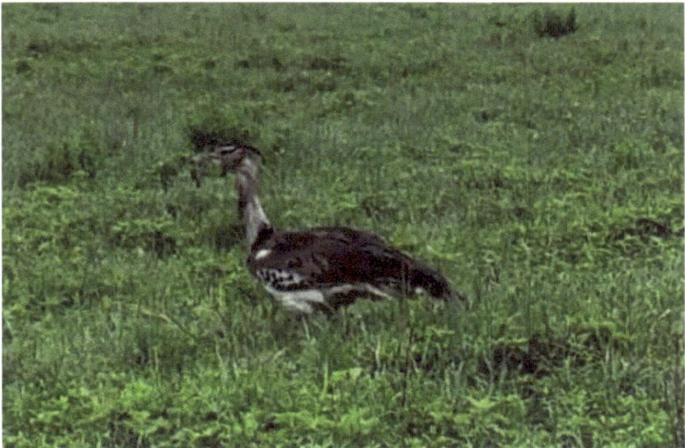

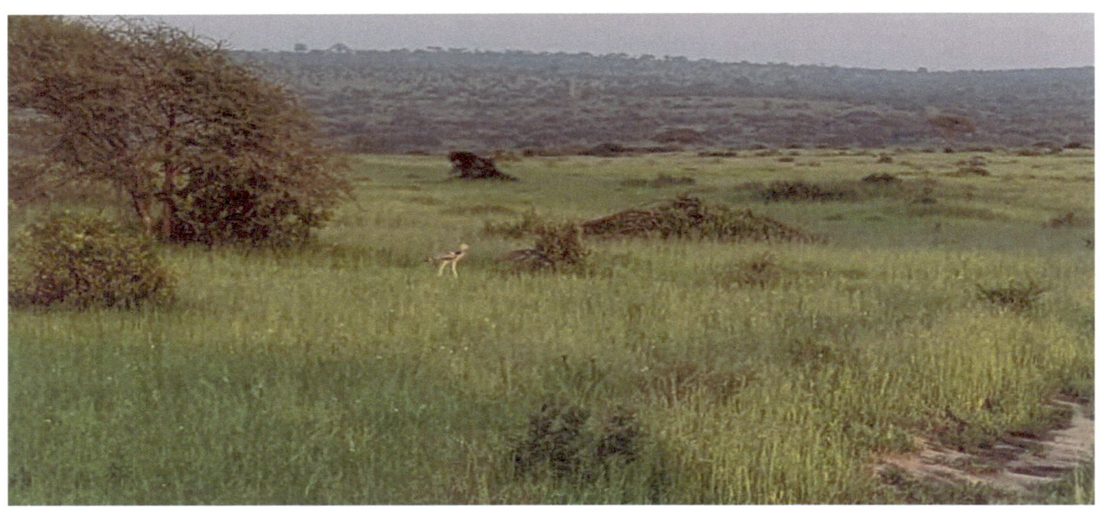

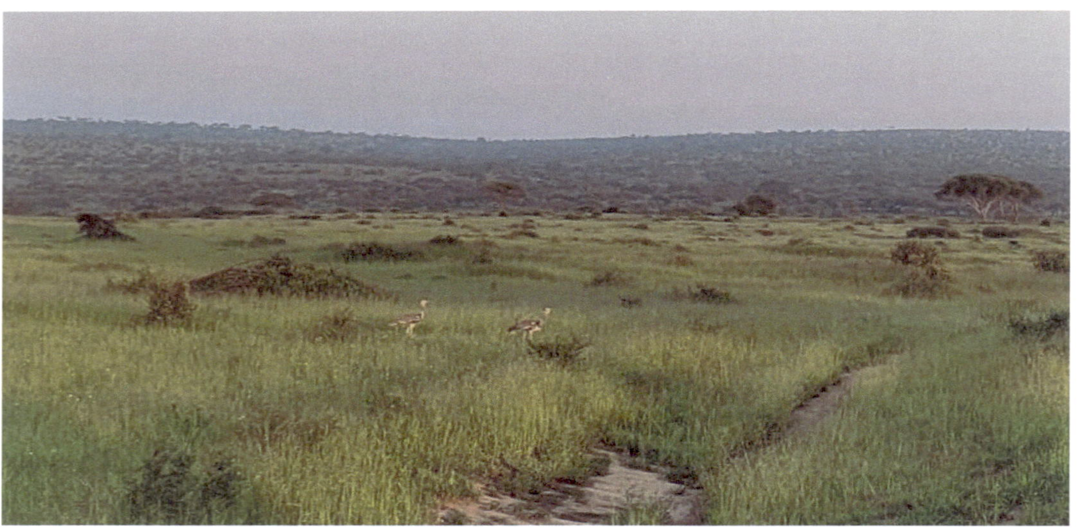

Tarangire N. P. is also home to the Cape Buffalo, one of the "Big Five" animals of the wild parks of East Africa (that makes 2 now, elephants and buffaloes). A collection of males, known admiringly as Buffalo Soldiers, is fearless of lions. They form a defense, facing outward to confront lions when they're around.

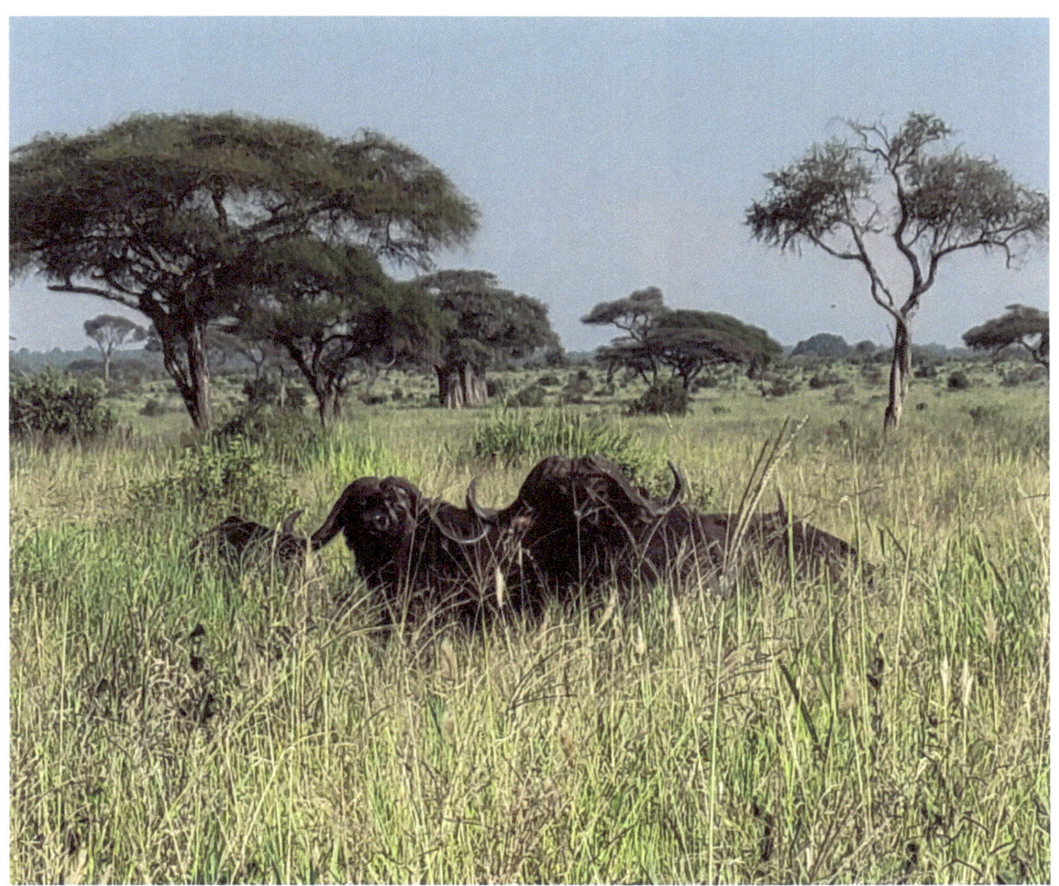

On the back of this Soldier is a mutualistic Yellow-billed Oxpecker (Buphagus africanus), a "passerine bird in the family Buphagidae, previously placed in the starling and myna family, Sturnidae".

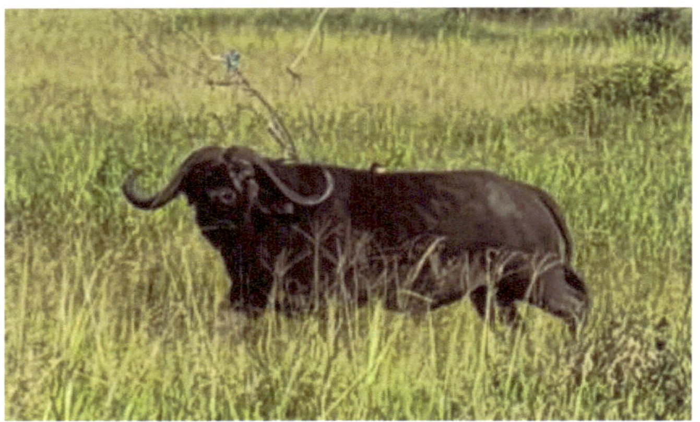

This mother Impala had her ears and nostrils alert to detect any dangers to the new calf that she gave birth to that Spring morning.

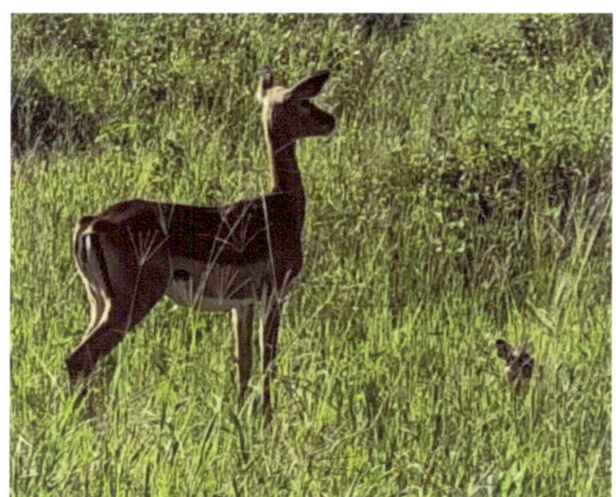

Evening light on the Tarangire N. P. Baobab and Acacia trees.

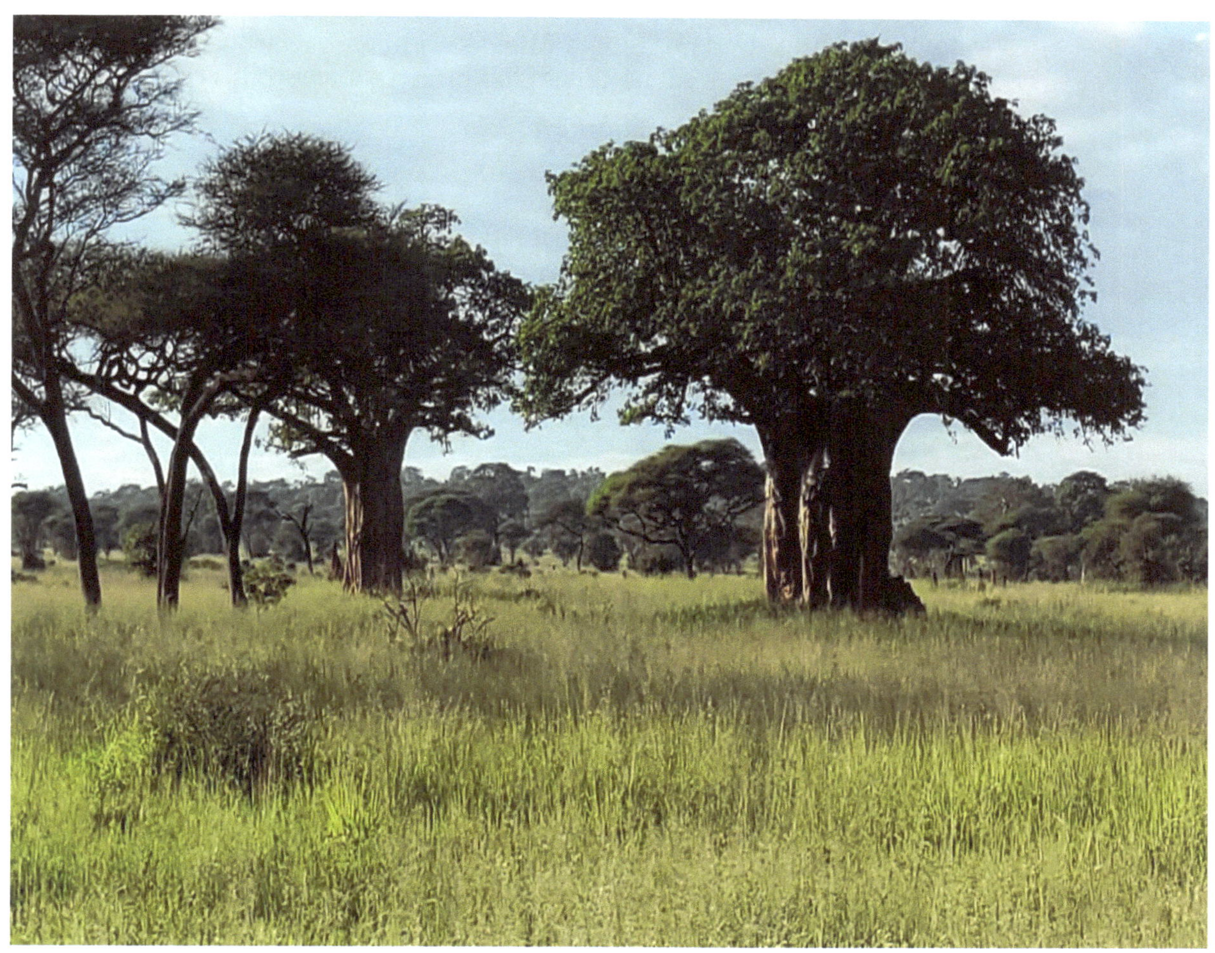

Our tour included a very pleasant, sunny brunch buffet at a picnic area, to let us experience getting out of the tour jeep and putting our feet on the morning ground. Afterwards, we ran into a band of young giraffes who were bonding and also sparring - it gets pretty rough.

Then, more sweet boys (one particularly young one), the Maasai Giraffes, in Tarangire N. P., feeding on thorny Acacia trees. They start with the leaves at the tips of the branches where it's not thorny, moving

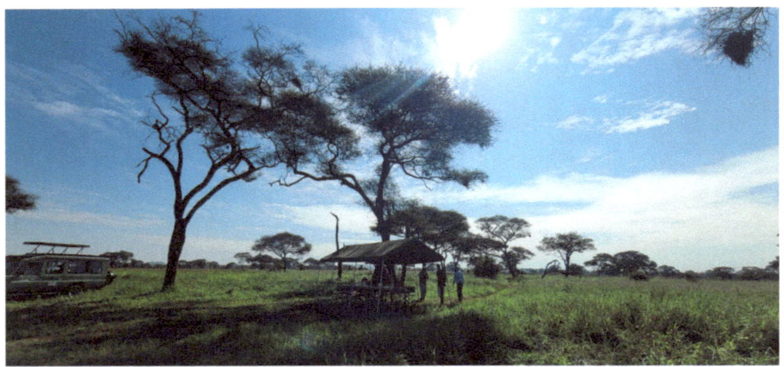

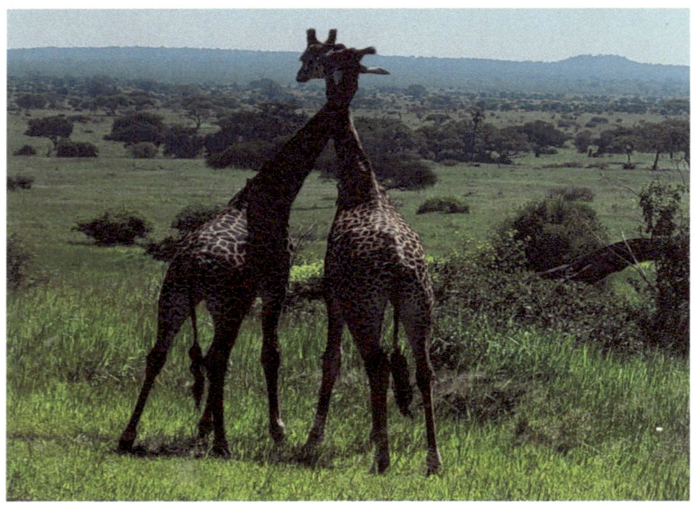

from one bush or tree to another to not build up on thorn toxins. Our wonderful guide described their technique of using their long thin tongues to work around Acacia thorns, and they have antiseptic saliva in case they encounter one. Evolution is amazing!

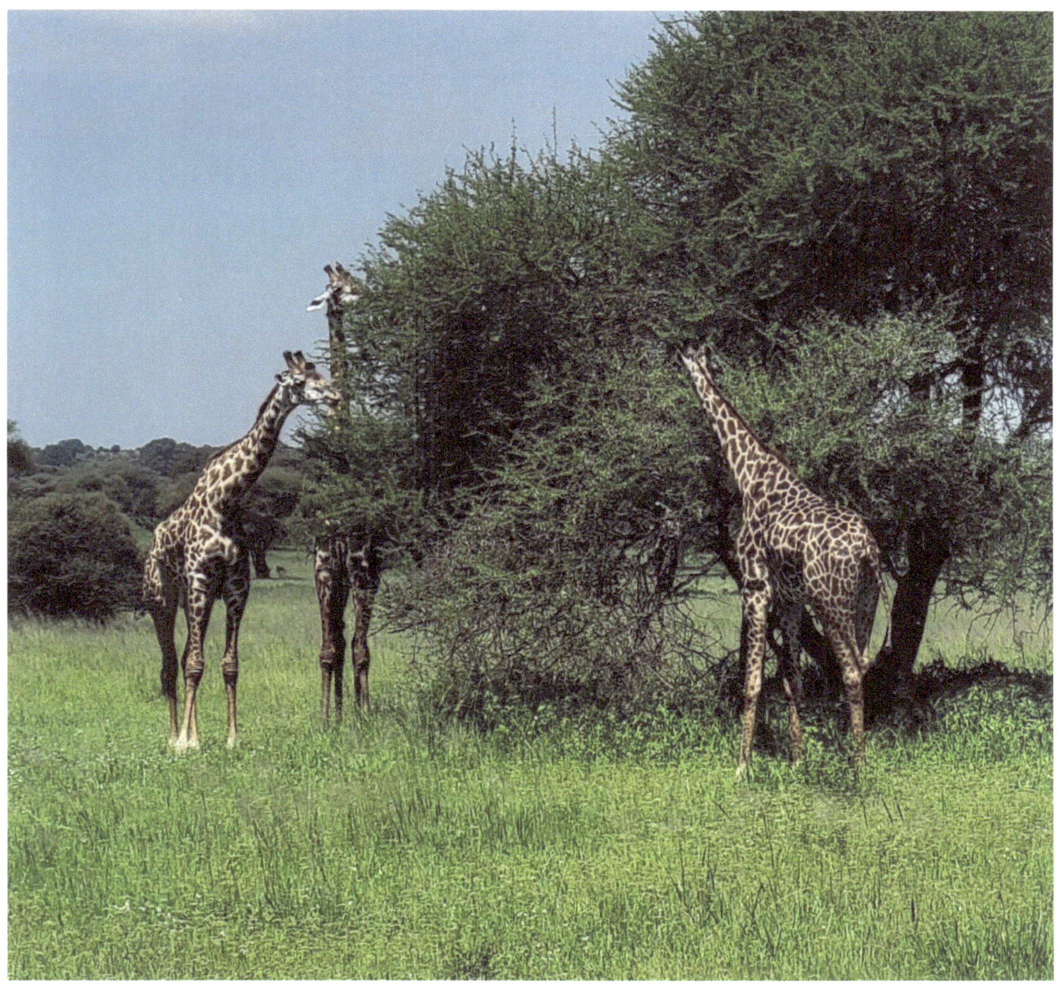

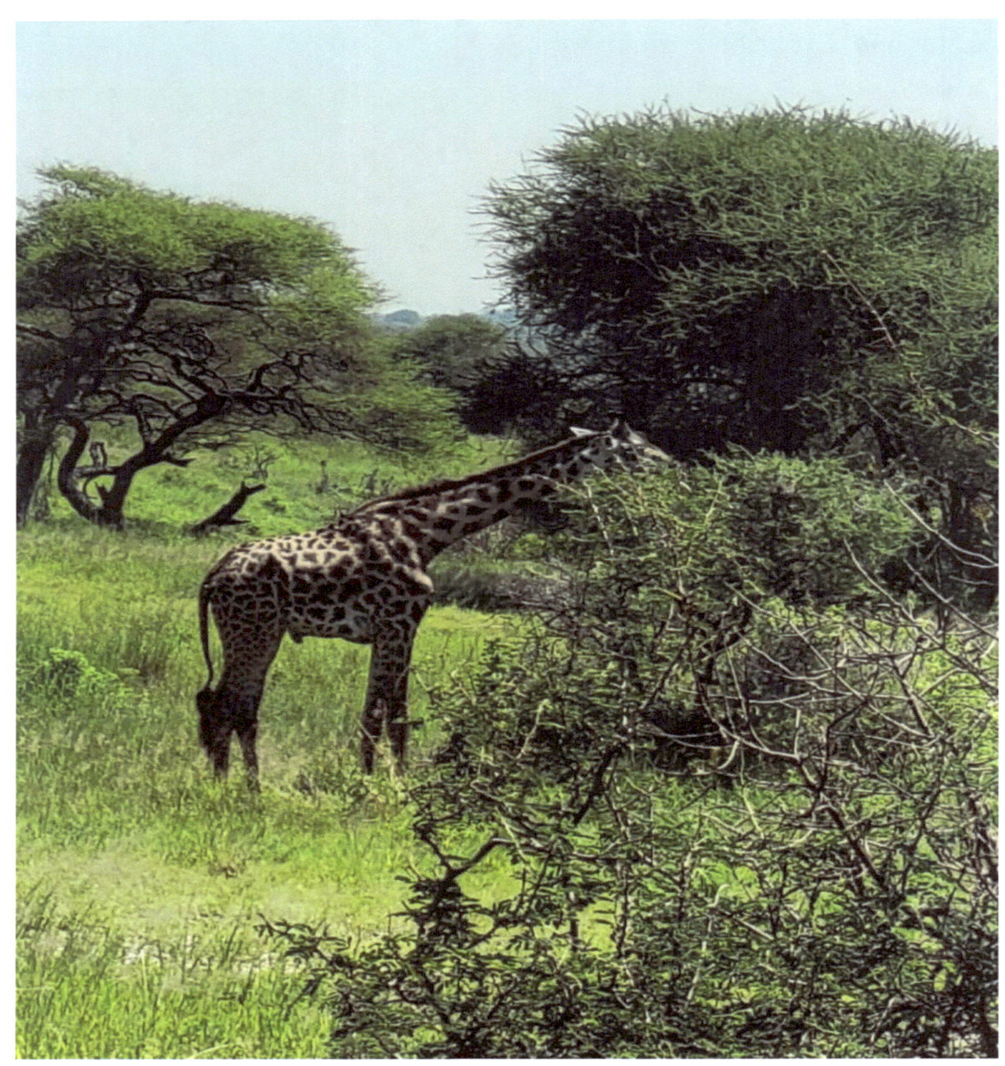

A nice view of Tarangire Mountain.

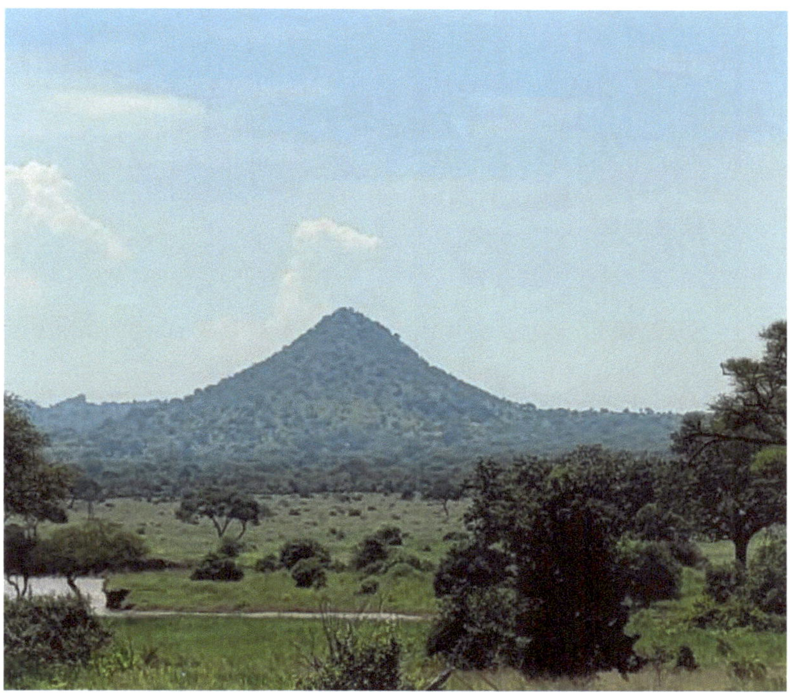

"The Tarangire River is a perennial river located in central Manyara Region in the eastern branch of the East African Rift Valley, within northern Tanzania."

"The headwaters of the Tarangire River are in the highlands and escarpments of Babati District of the Manyara Region and Kondoa District of the Dodoma Region, primarily the Irangi Hills and Irangi Escarpment in Kondoa District. The river originates in the Wasi Highlands, falls down the eastern Kondoa Escarpment" (for those who enjoy a little geography); it's a land of old volcanoes and fault lines (for those who like geology).

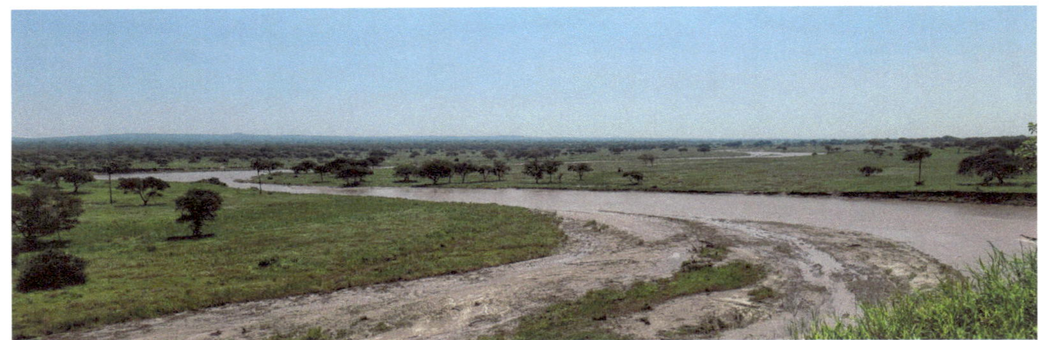

The safari (journey) guide said we're lucky to see the Tarangire N. P. elephants because they are migrating before the rainy season.

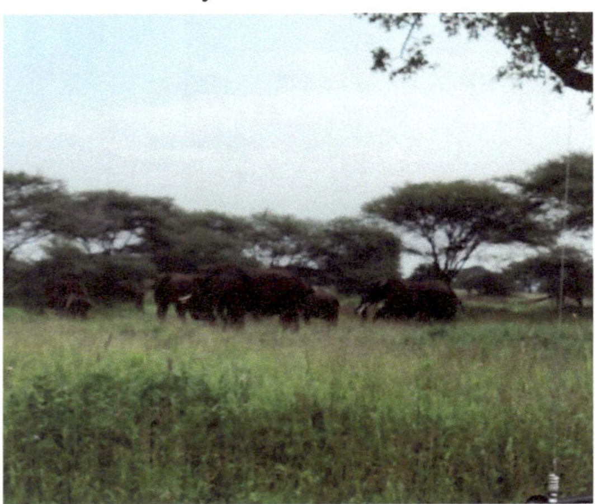

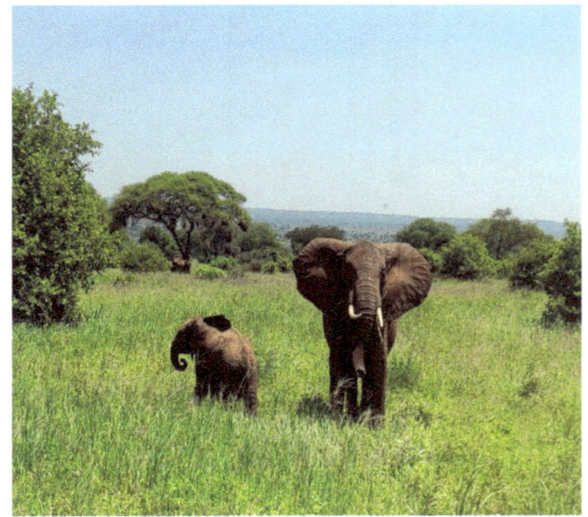

Notice the bull elephant in the bushes who approached the jeep; he was a little unnerving. Our guide assured us we were ok because there were not any females in estrus around, determined by the lack of urine running down a bull elephant's legs.

The large Waterbuck Antelopes of East Africa have white "toilet seat" rings around their tails.

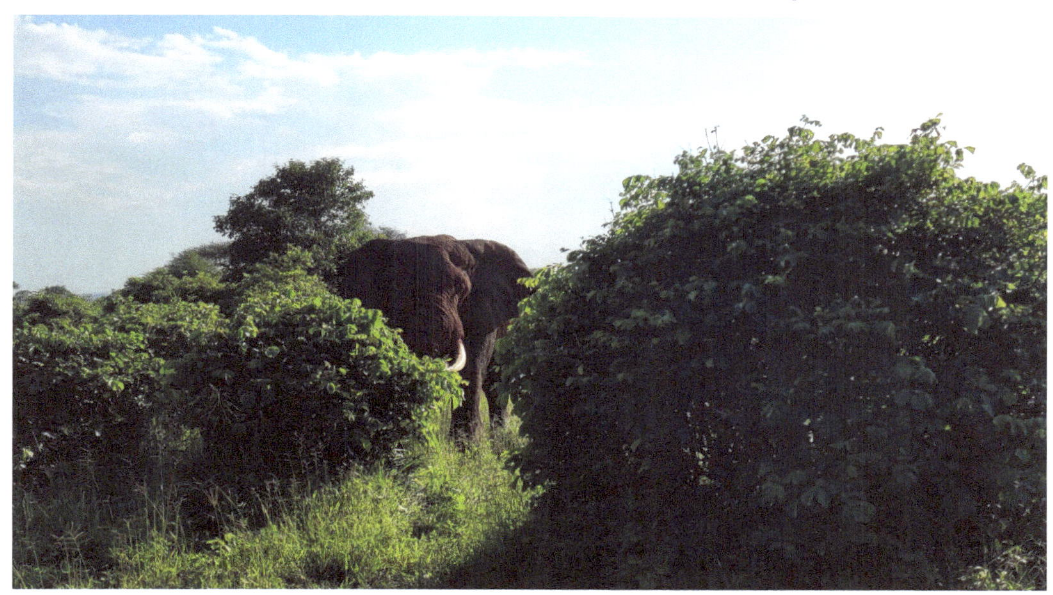

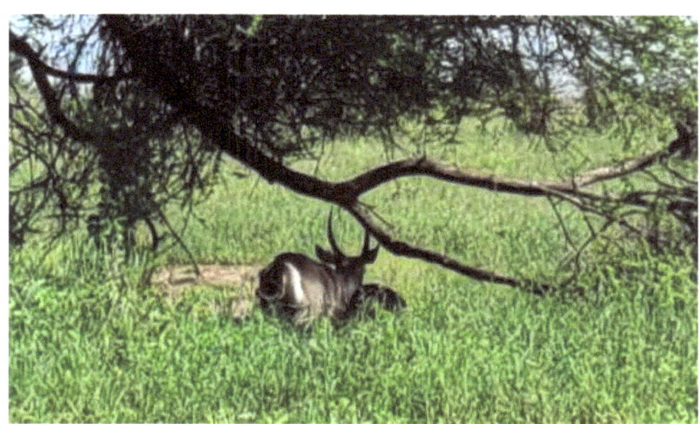

Market Day

After leaving Tarangire N. P. on Saturday, we passed a weekend "farmers market" (Wednesdays and Saturdays are market days).

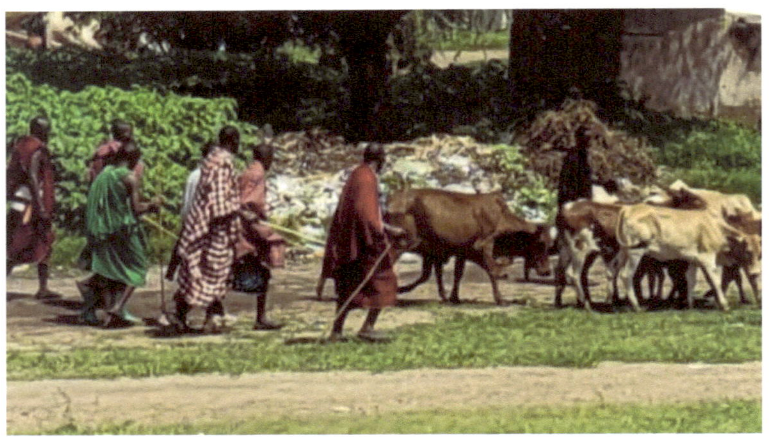

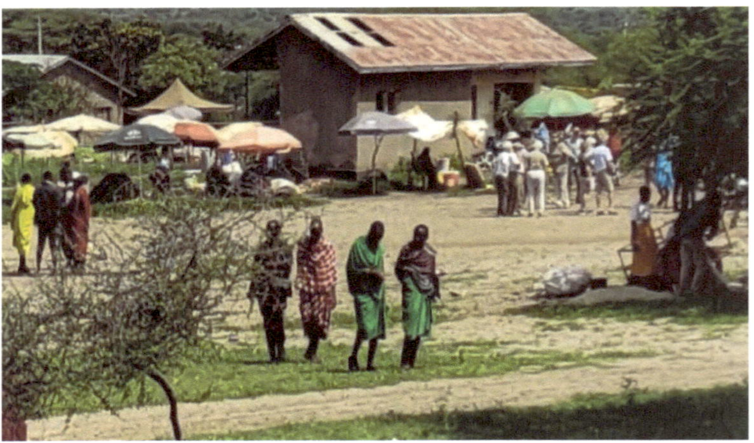

18

This day was centered around a livestock market and "stalls" were set up all around, similar to our pop-up farmer's market at our local urban park. The Maasai Tribe men, in red usually, bring their livestock. They prefer Zebu cows, similar to Brahman cows, because of their ability to tolerate the dry season.

Maasai Tribe men gathered around a livestock pen for the morning auction.

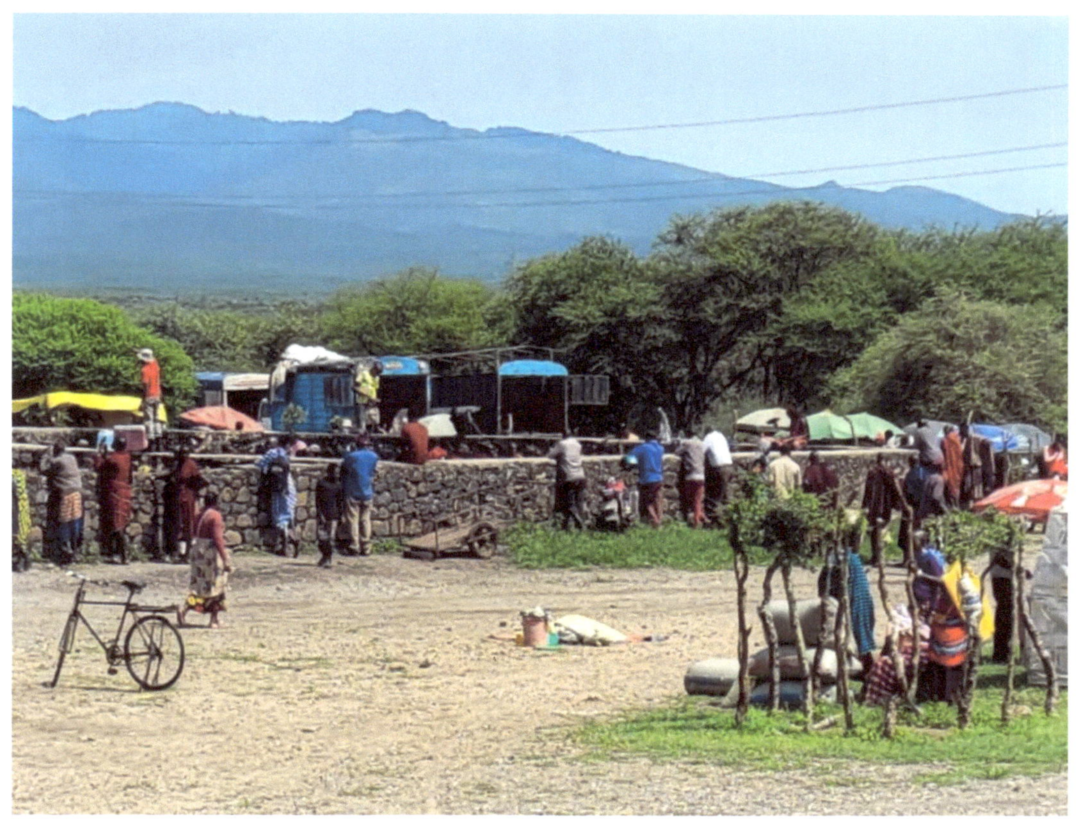

There are options for bus transportation, motorcycle taxis, and walking to market. See the outdoor cafe with tables on the right side and a lumber store for the boom in building. Vendors have brought crops, the much-needed Spring rain season boots, luggage, furniture and many other items.

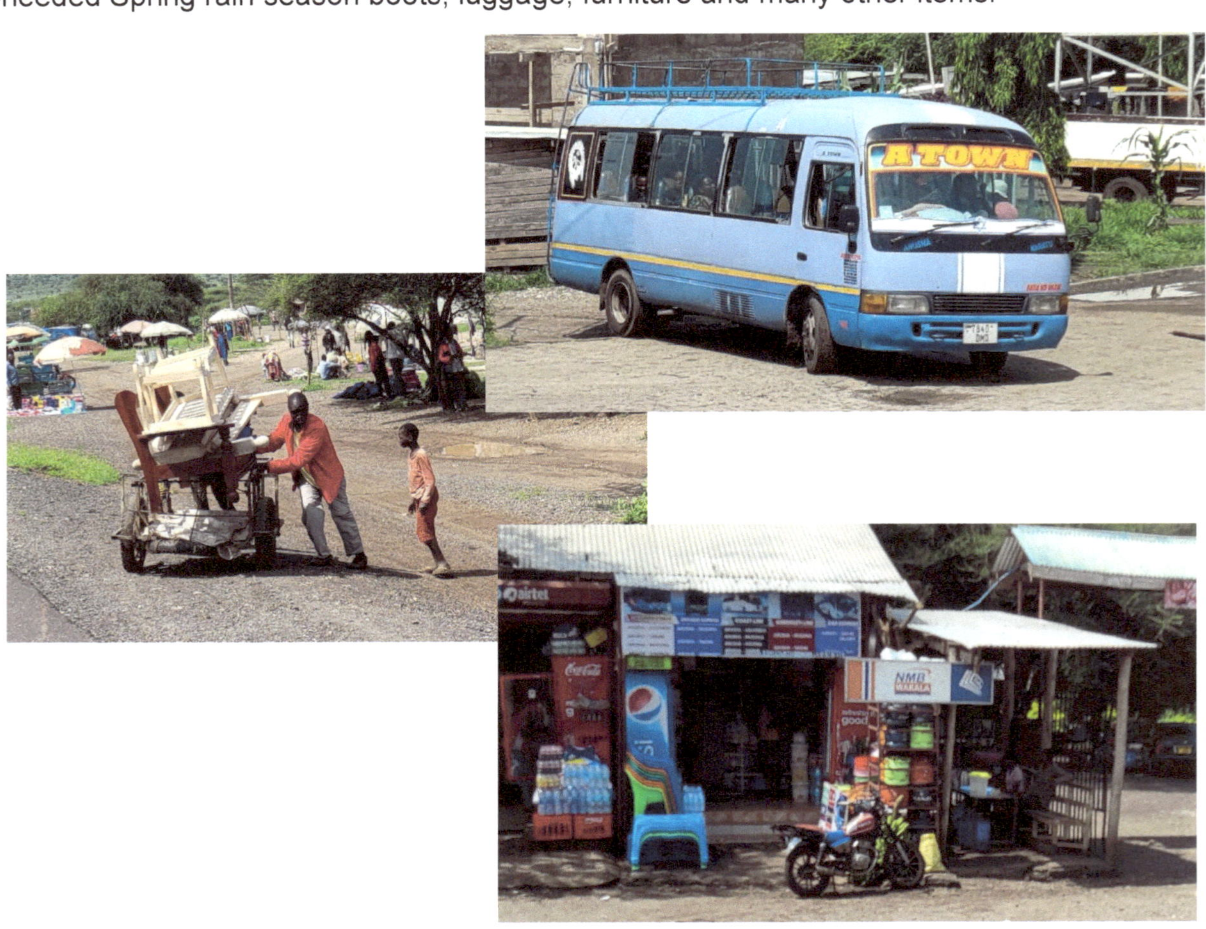

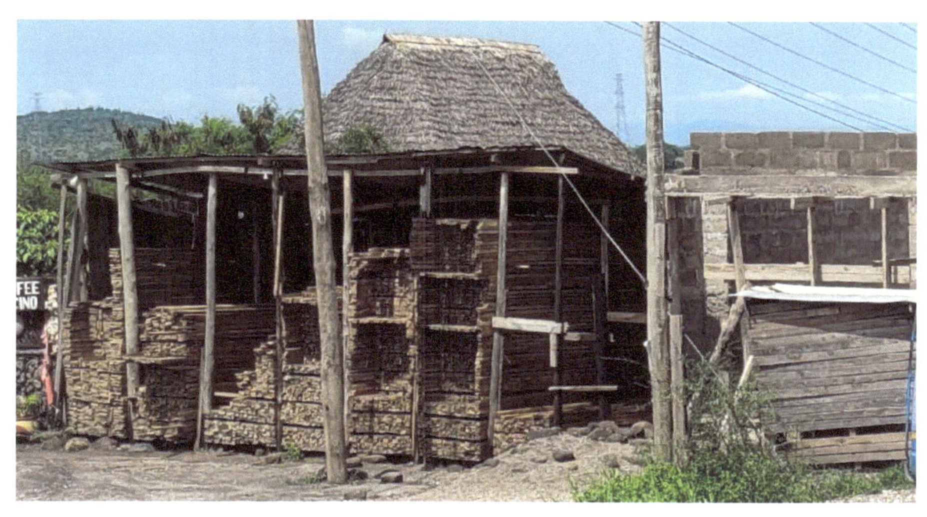

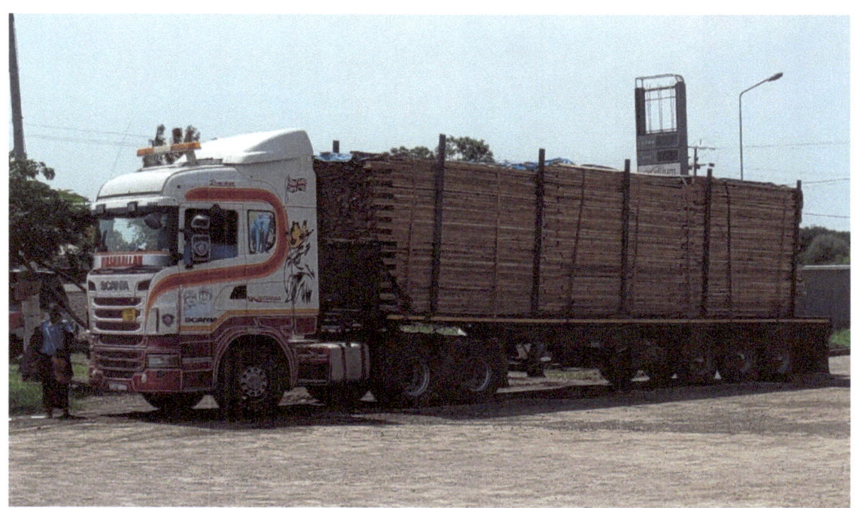

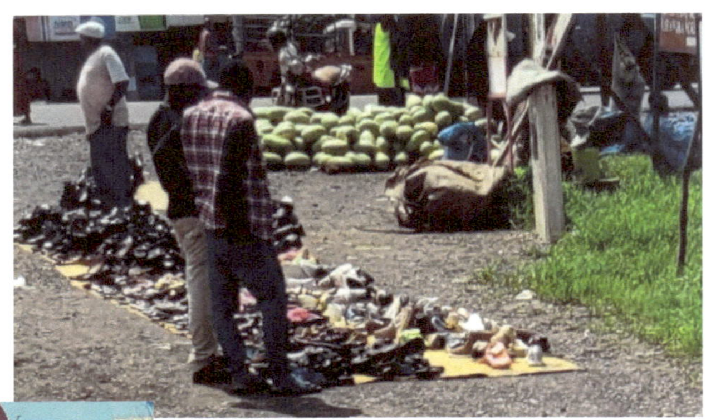

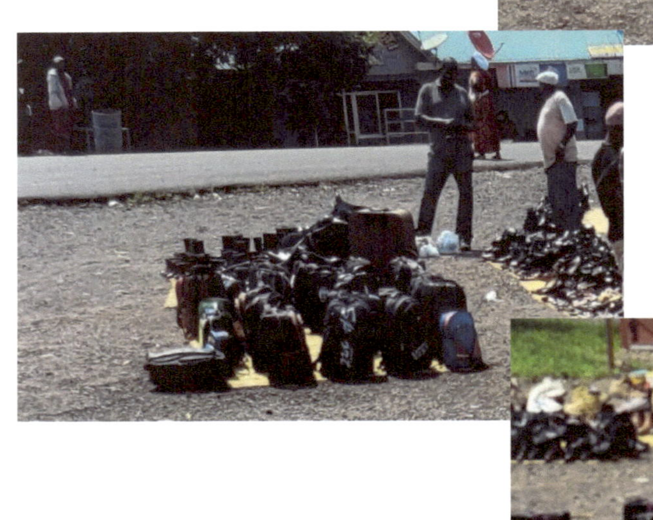

60% of Tanzanians are Christians due to the decades of control by the colonial British Empire. The writing in the front of the Fort Jesus van is Swahili, the language of East Africa, and it says God's Blessings (God's Grace).

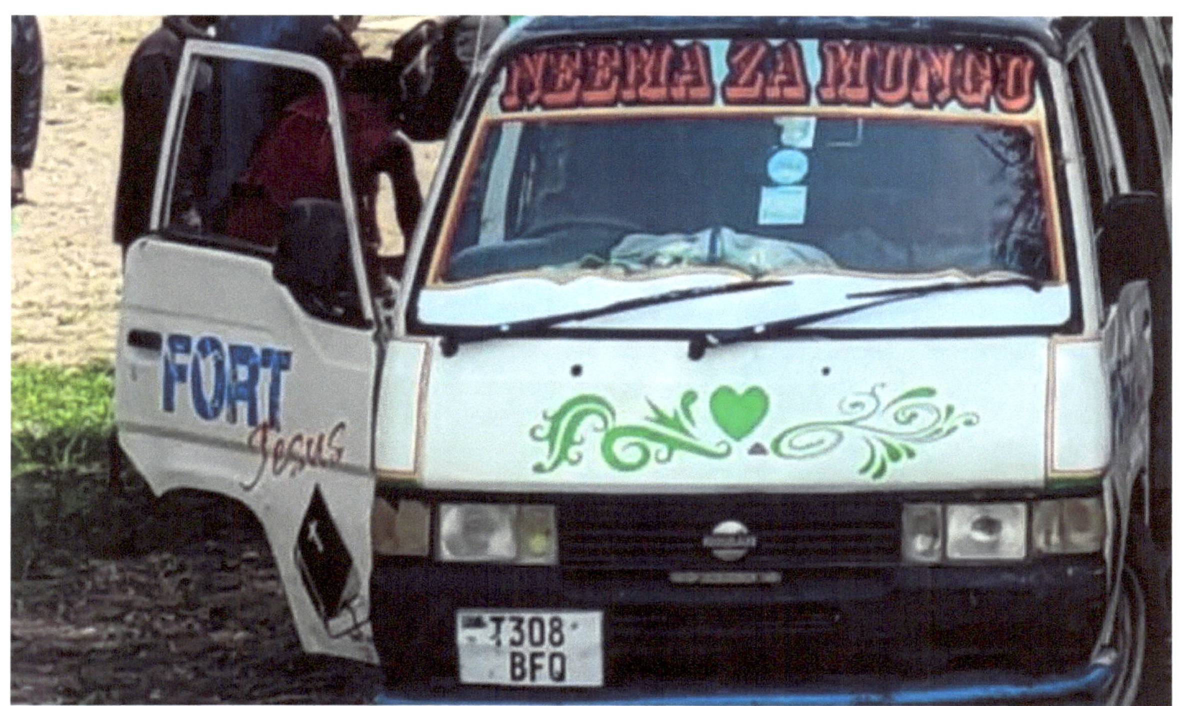

Lake Manyara

Easy travel to Lake Manyara - no restrictions on clothes colors, meaning red, was ok since we wouldn't be encountering lions who distrust rural Maasai lion hunters who wear red. At least they used to. Now the government compensates the Maasai for livestock lost to lions in exchange for ending hunting. The lions didn't get the memo; the lions still don't trust red and tell their cubs not to either.

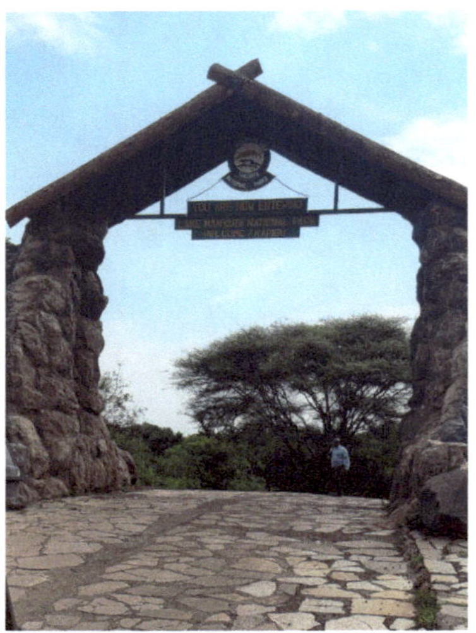

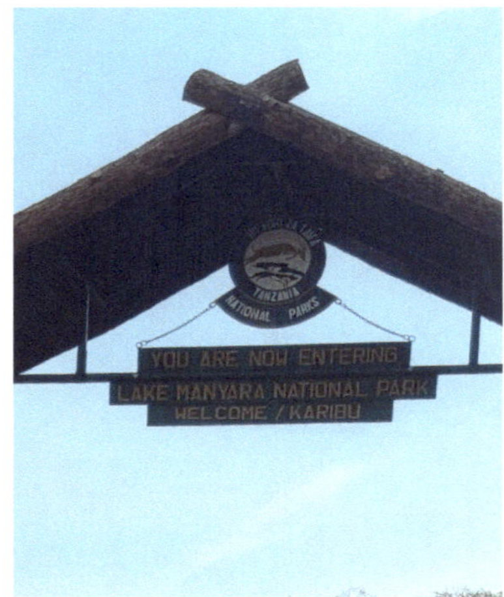

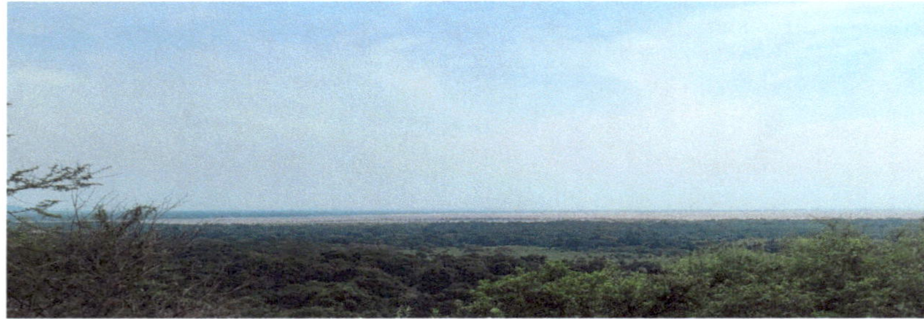

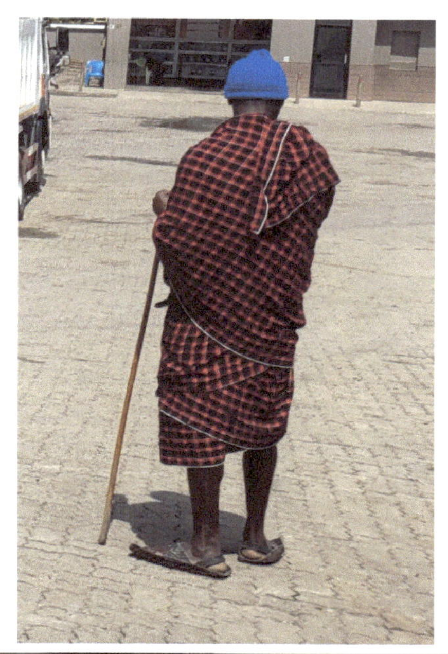

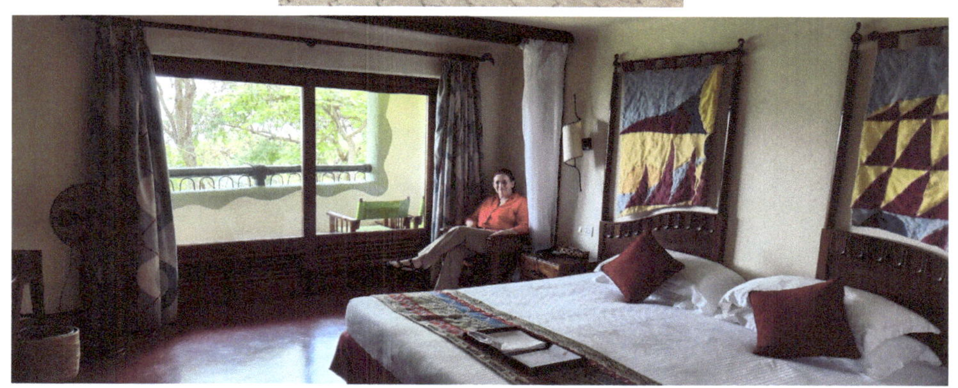

Local high school students from the Lake Manyara area are hired to perform drumming, singing and acrobatics for visitors who gather in the evening for drinks and hors d'oeuvre on the lawn overlooking the lake valley below.

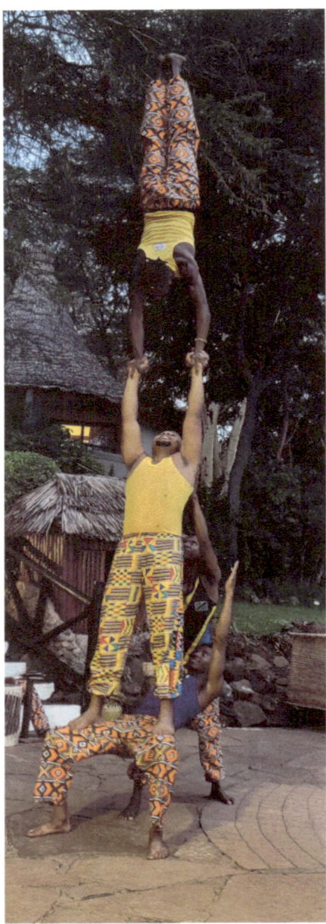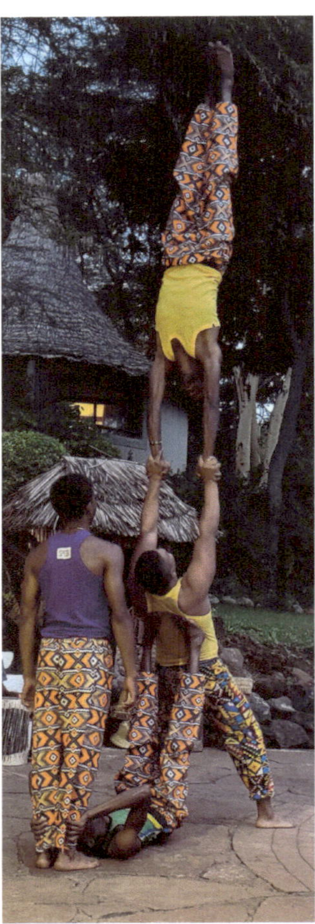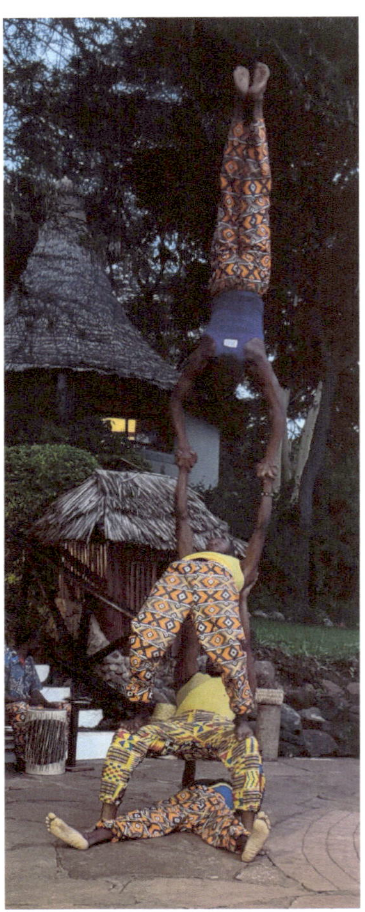

Lake Manyara N. P. elephants were coming through the forest so we stopped to watch. A male was checking out all of the females (not his lucky day). The female holding her right leg up was using this technique to stop, study and collect important information. A fascinating experience for all of us.

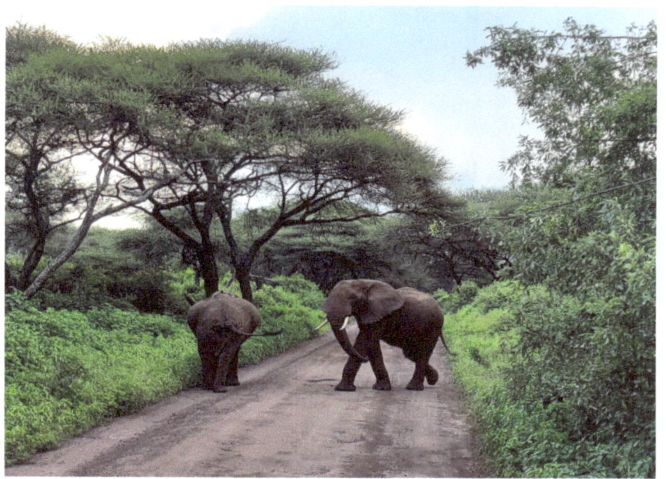

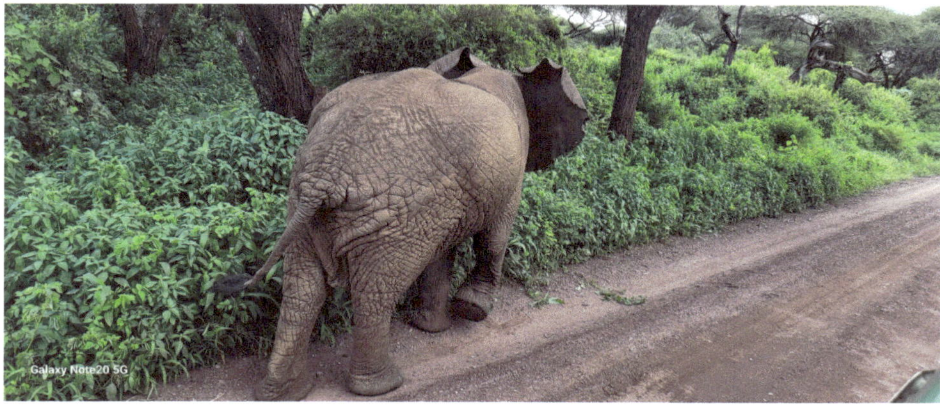

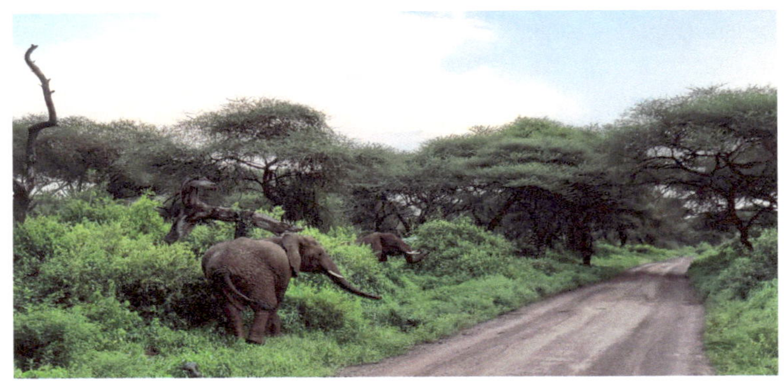

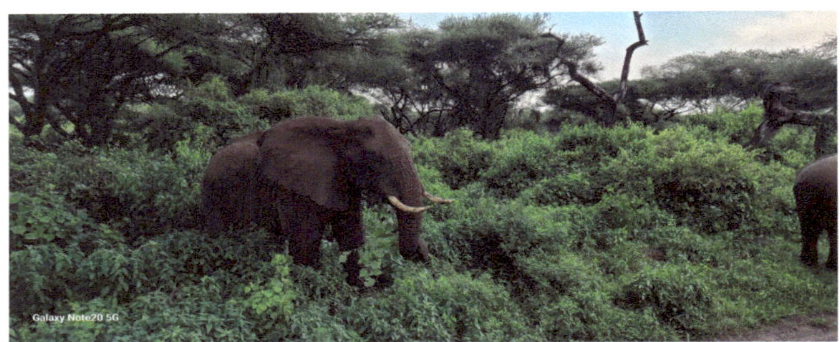

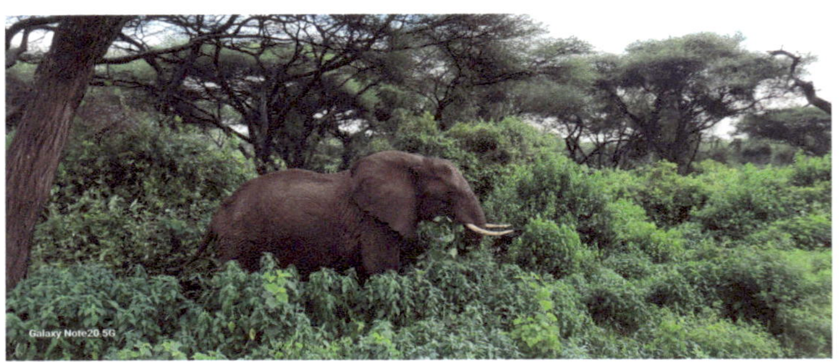

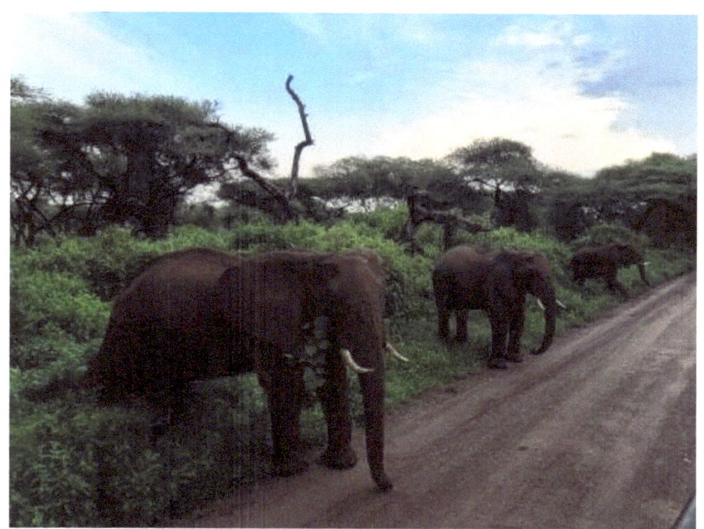

The next page photo, however, takes the cake for me, because apparently elephants have an interest in red, too, on occasion, and this ellie was growing a bit nervous when she came down the mountain path and through the bushes, then saw bright red me standing up in the jeep, taking her picture. Our guide saw her alarm, waving her ear, and he abruptly instructed me to sit down - and I was happy to oblige! She was satisfied. We learned that the elephant is the most dangerous animal in Africa, and got our first-hand lesson very quickly.

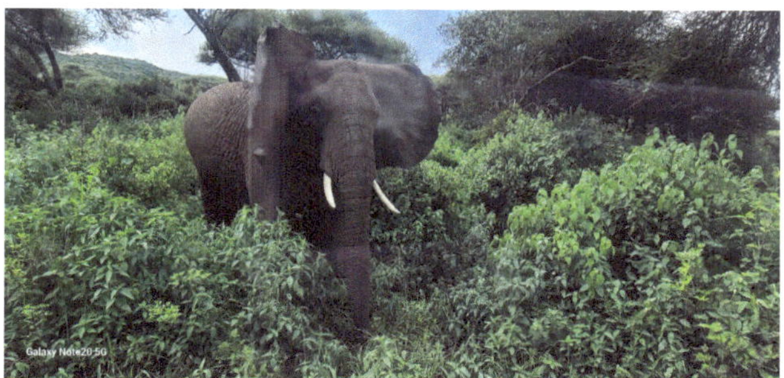

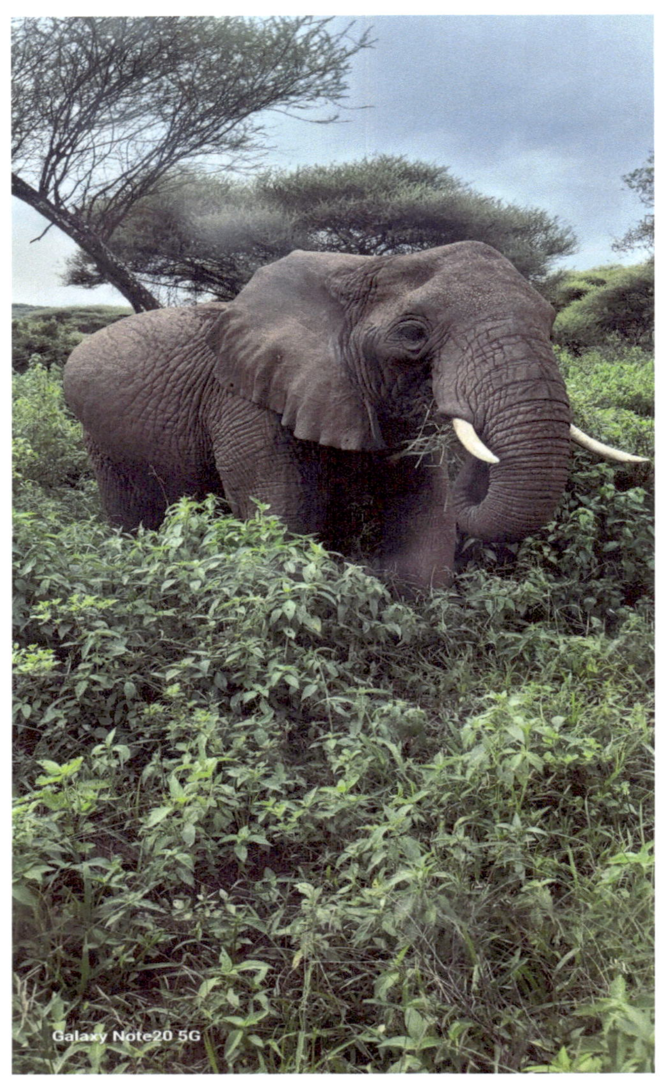
Galaxy Note20 5G

Yellow-bark Acacia "Fever Trees" at Lake Manyara were preserved, saved from destruction by elephants, when Douglas I. Hamilton developed a tree conservation strategy in the 1950s of wrapping them in wire cages. End of problem and now they flourish.

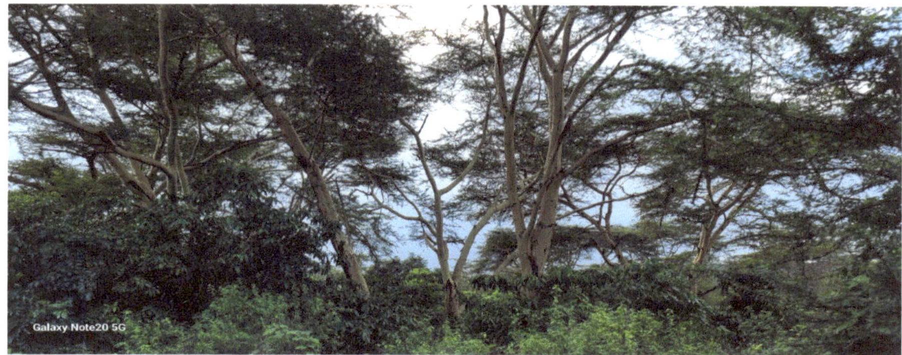

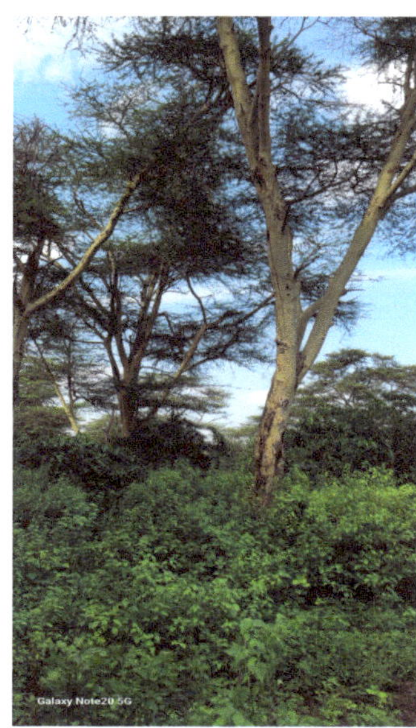

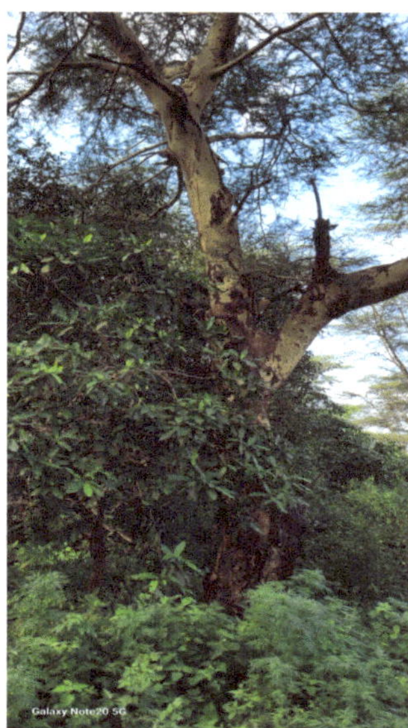

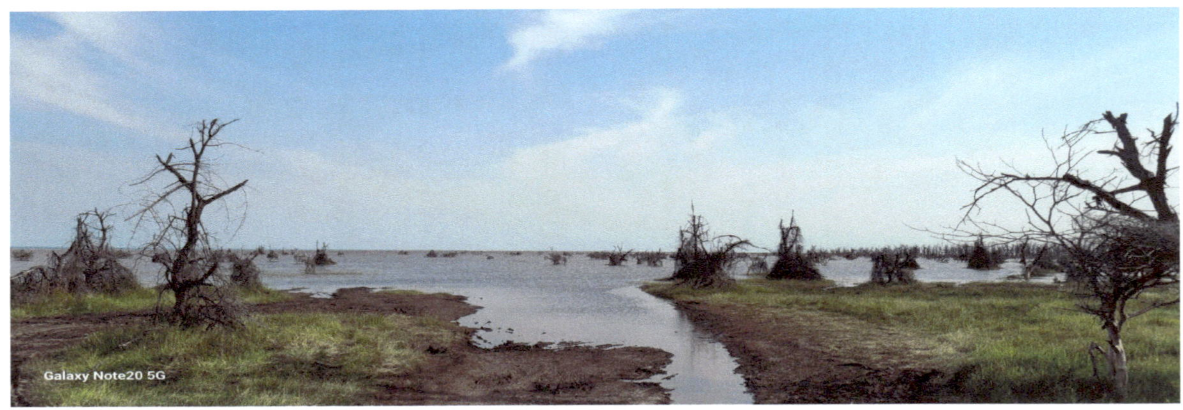

Unlike many others, our guide is a trained and life-long passionate naturalist with details on everything you want to know - like, is that elephant going to charge us? ("Not today bc ...) What about that lion? "He's just looking for his brothers". Oh, and "that little white flower is Clandestina".

A troop of baboon females and infants were relaxing near the road, until they noticed racket up the hill created by the lead male scolding a juvenile who was harassing a young member exploring the trees.

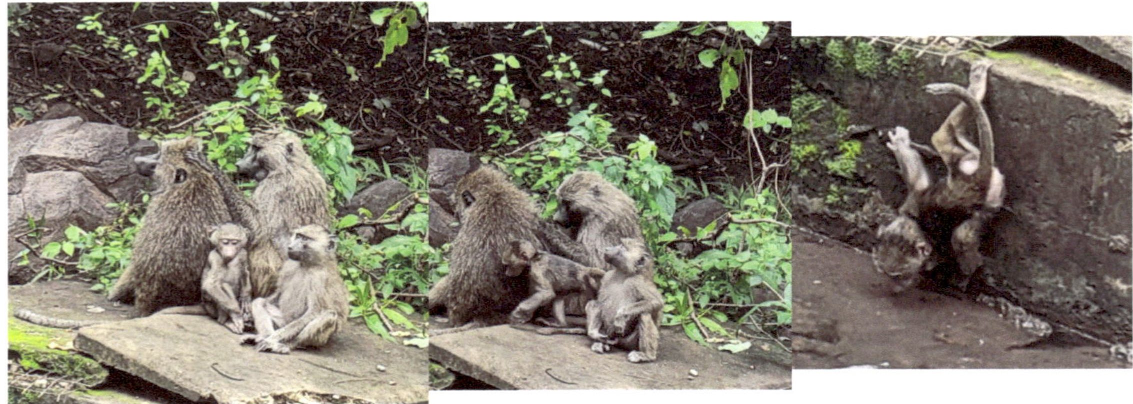

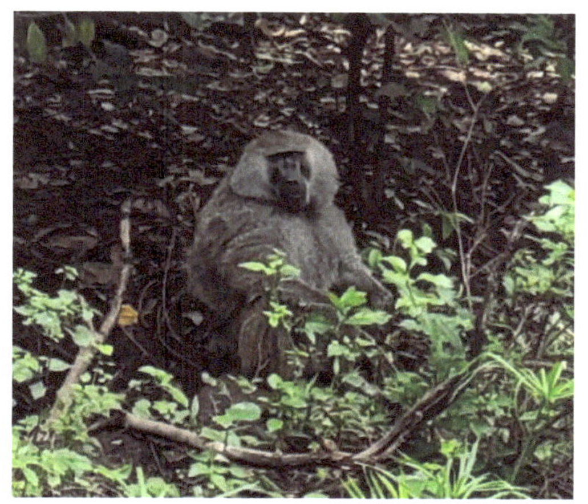

A pair of Blue Monkeys at Lake Manyara.

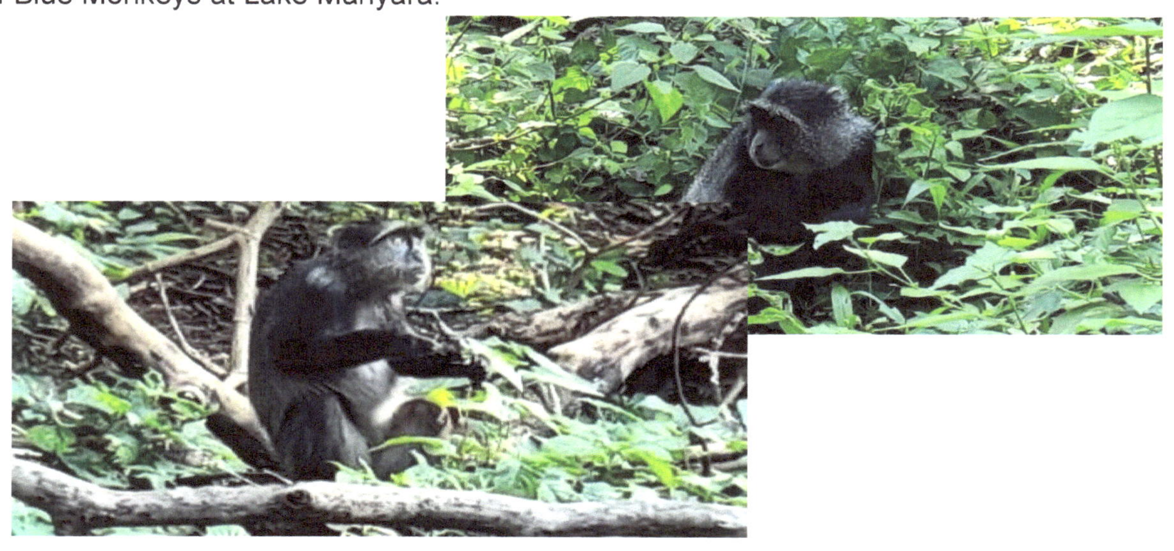

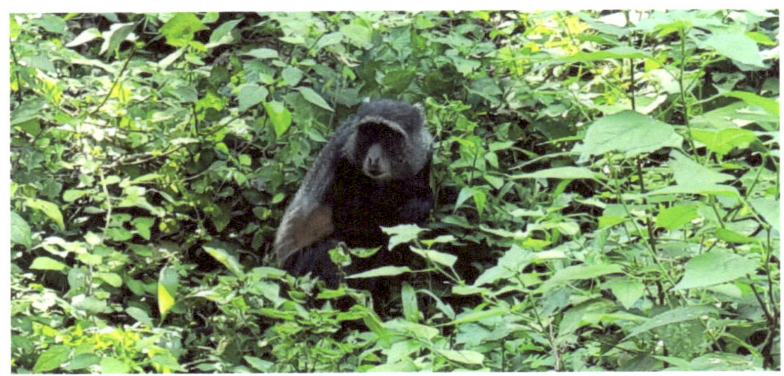

At Lake Manyara the monkeys were enjoying Vine Fruit and Wild Mangoes.

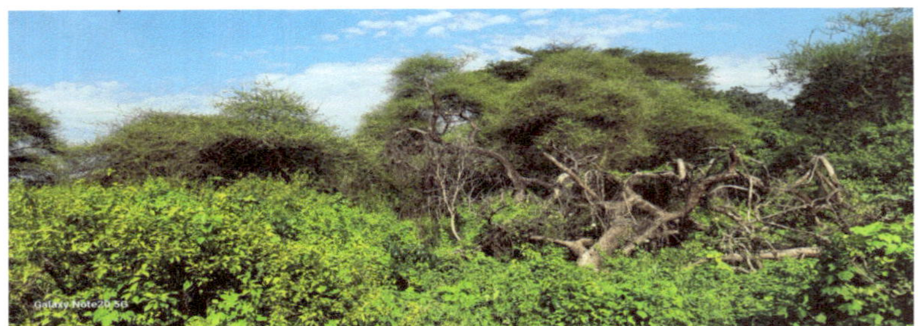

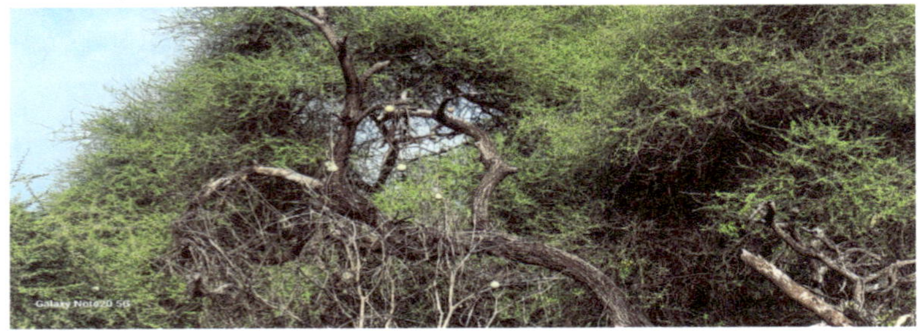

Gibb's Farm

With our tour guide at Gibb's Farm, we toured the entire organic garden, then had a farm-to-table lunch on the patio (while he took a well-derserved break from guide duties).

We were invited for our walking tour to use a walking stick made from the Elephant Perfume tree (Klaudia aneseta) that elephants like to rub against.

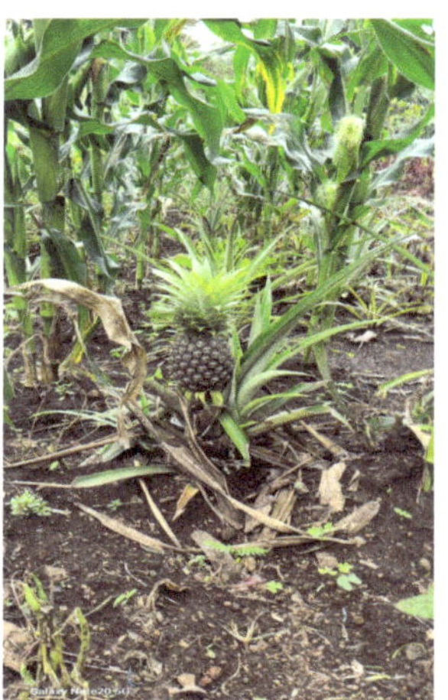 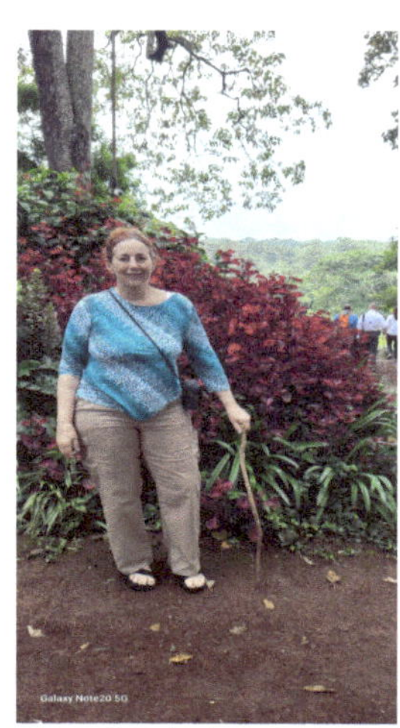 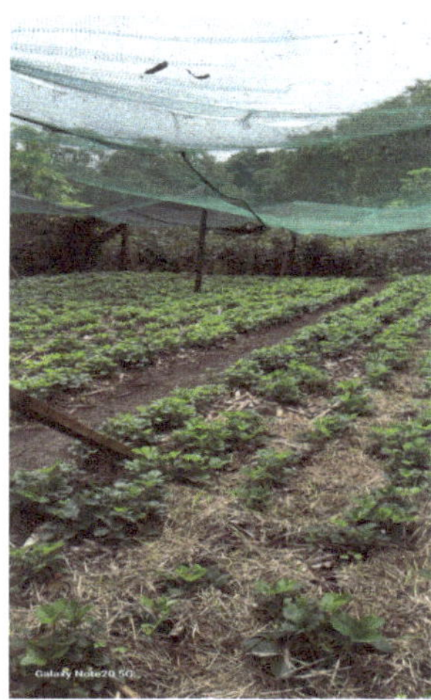

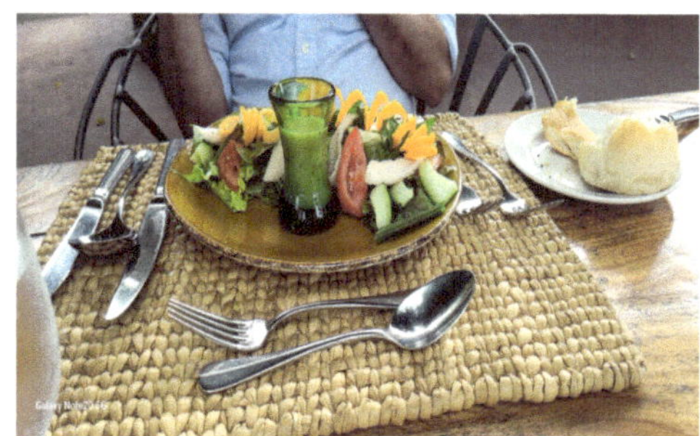

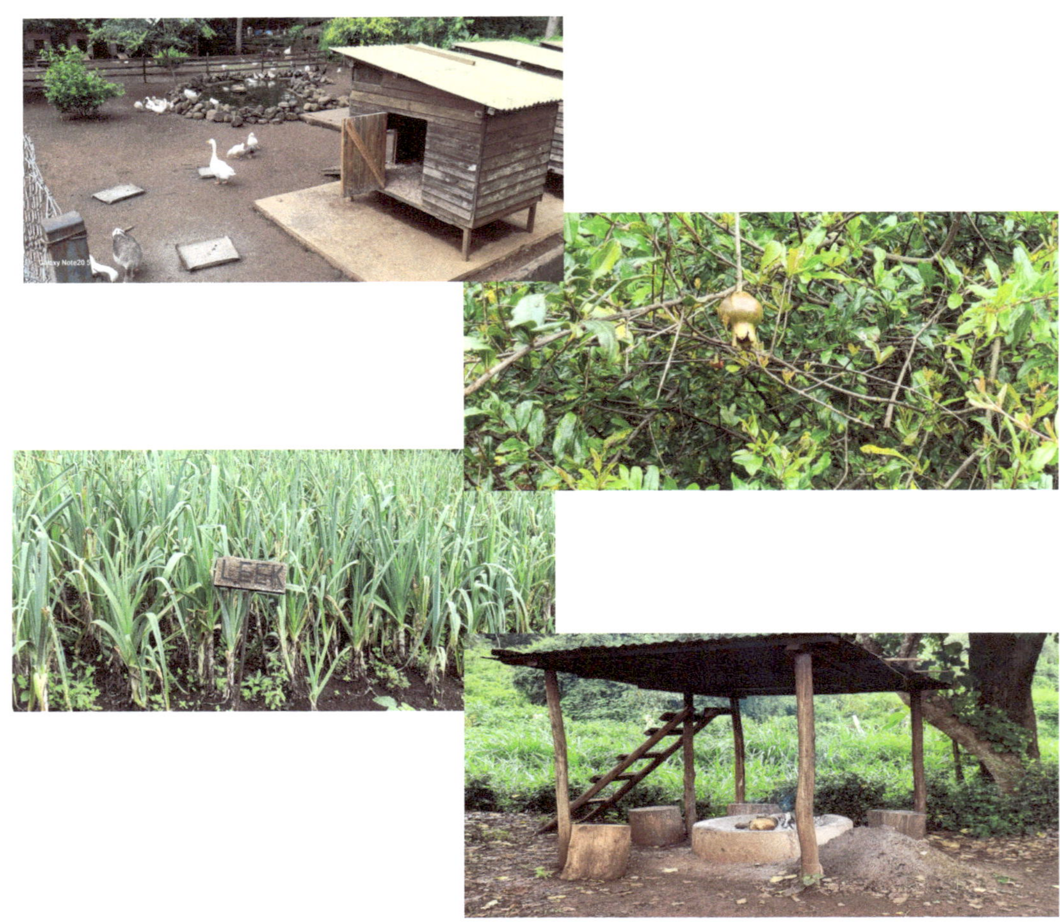

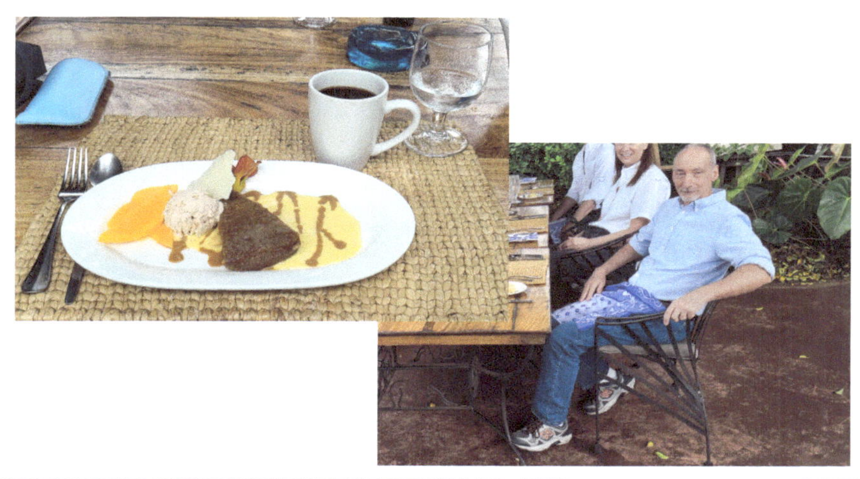

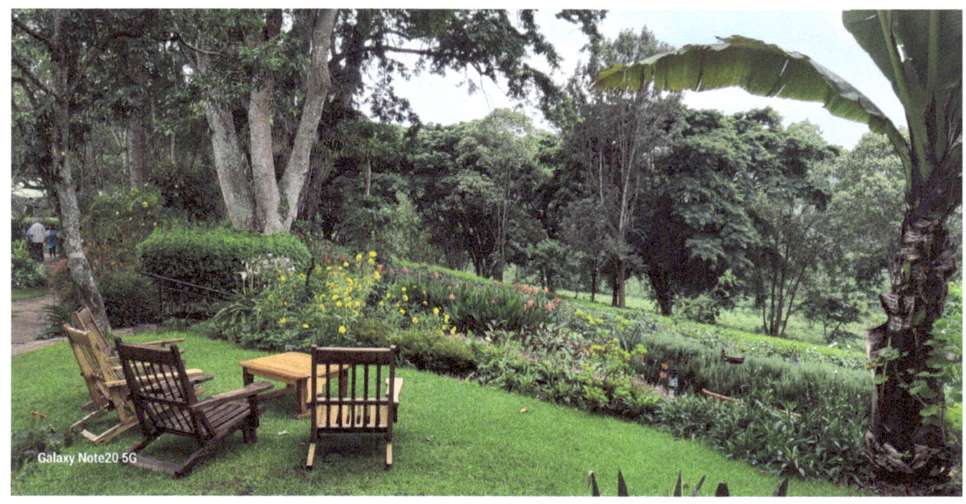

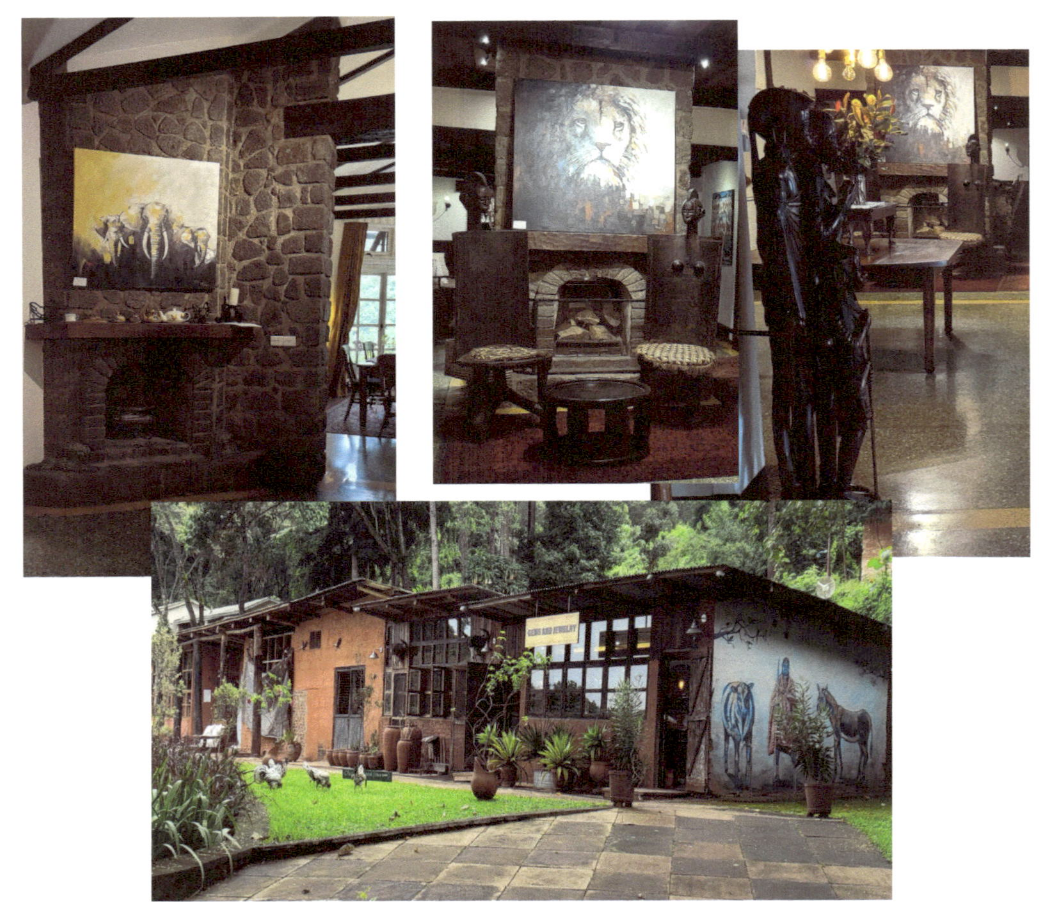

A gallery of artwork was in the main home, now serving as offices, gathering space and possibly some lodging, while another area of the Gibb property was built to serve as a row of shops and a resort.

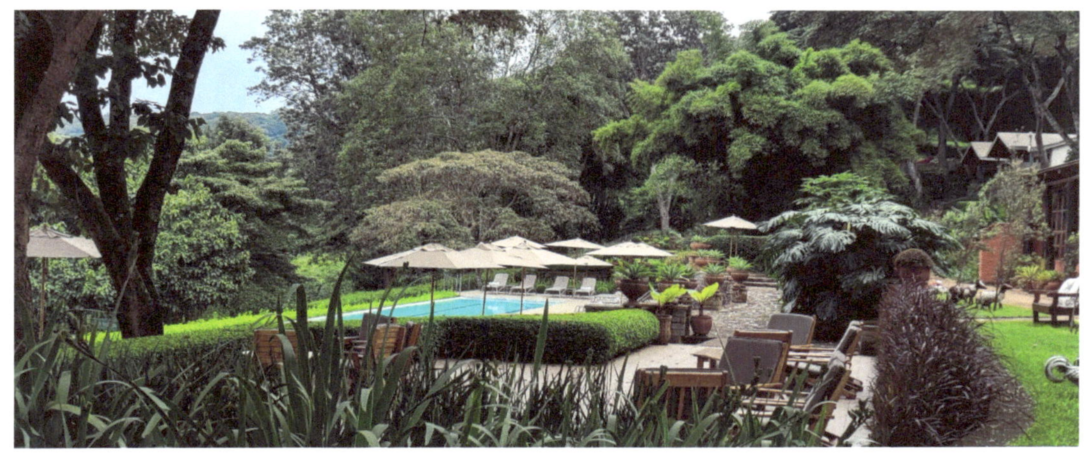

Satiated and ready to go, our band took off for the next adventure - the trip to the Ngorongoro Crater.

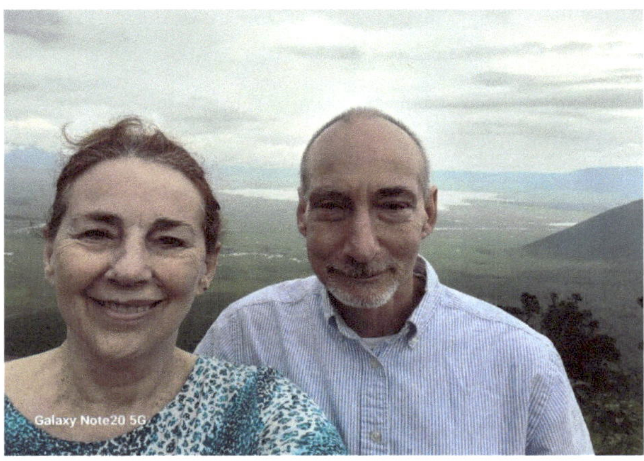

Ngorongoro Crater (Caldera) Conservation Area

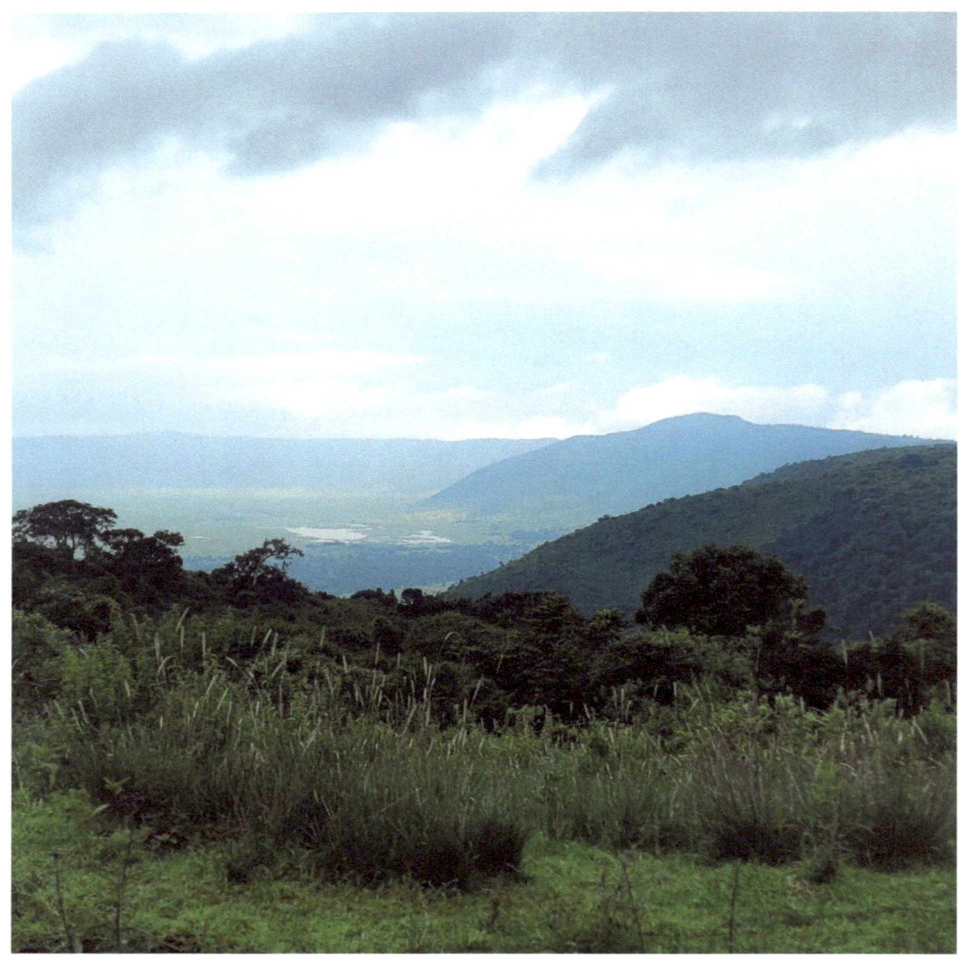

40

From the rim of the Ngorongoro Crater.

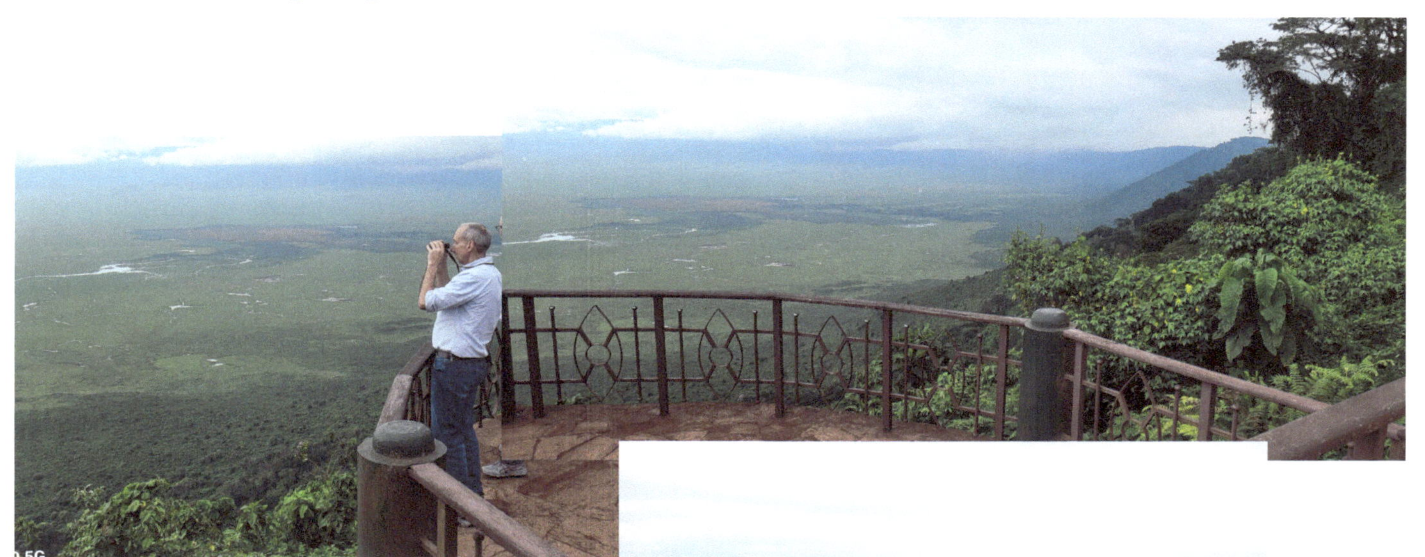

41

Ngorongoro Serena Lodge (Ngorongoro Conservation Area / Caldera "Crater" rim, 2,000 ft. above the Crater).

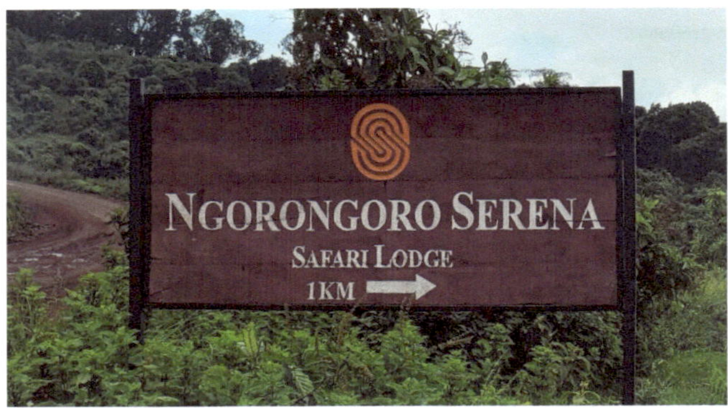

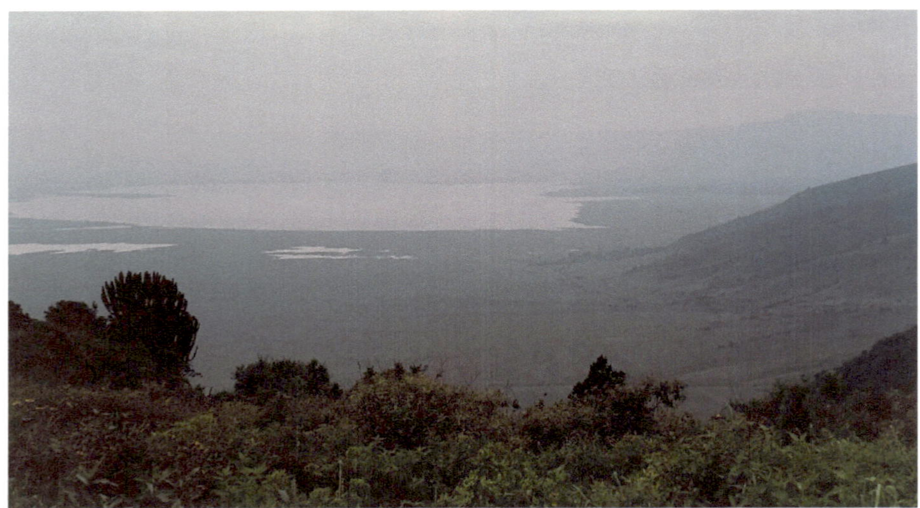

We were greeted by a local Maasai Tribe group who were hired to sang and danced traditional songs in the lobby and on the veranda. It was a real treat for those of us who enjoy singing and dancing.

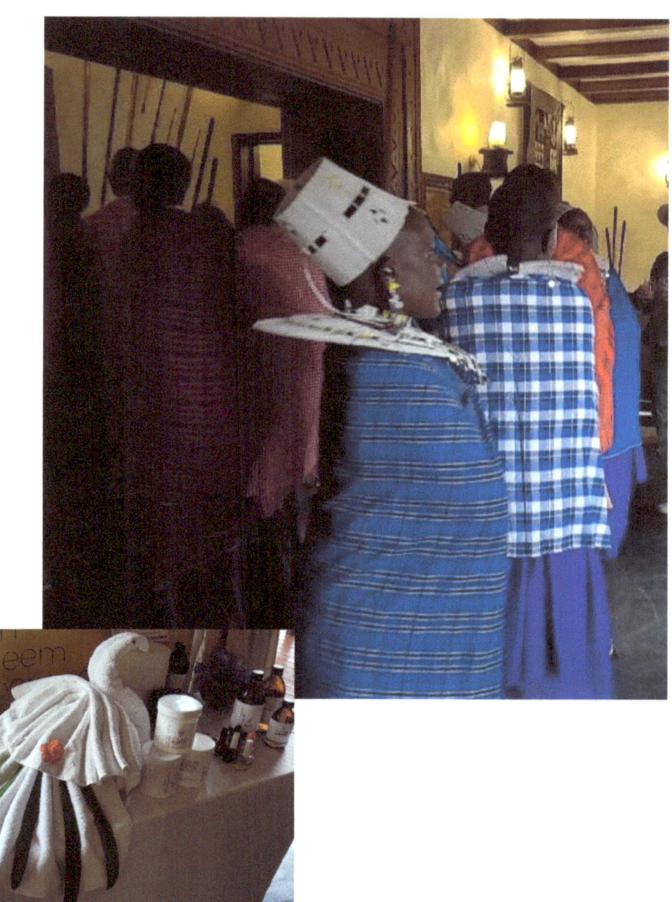

In the morning, we met two female young lion sisters hanging out and playing in the quarry, our guide assured us that Mom was nearby, possibly hunting or resting. The quarry equipment was part of their playground. I'm sure the workers hadn't arrived yet or found something else to do for awhile.

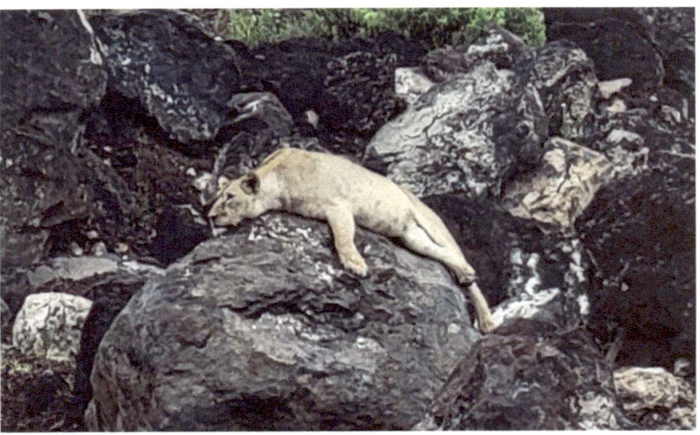

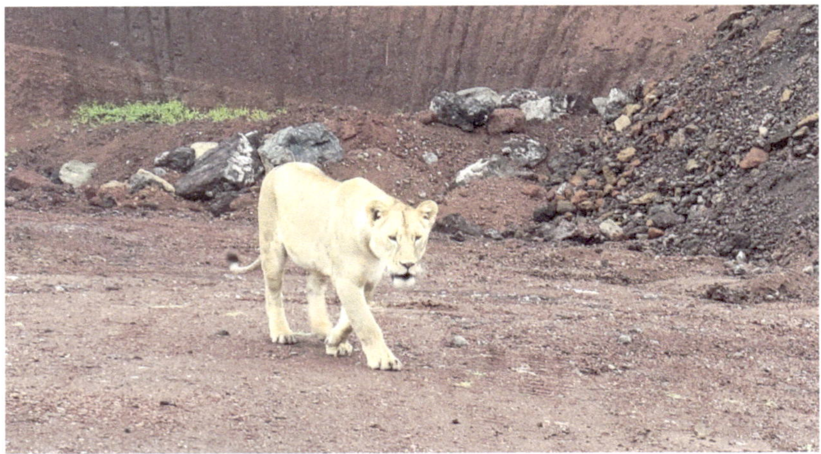

It was pretty thrilling when one of the girls came over to explore the jeep and sneaked up on us from behind. We were taking pictures of the other one and turned our heads to find the sister standing next to the jeep starting straight up at us. The guide was watching her and when she turned her attention to playing with the tires, he slowly backed up to discourage a possible, and definitely unwanted, tire puncture. Meanwhile, I love the shots I got of the sister whose only interest was going to play with her now awake sister-on-the move (our jeep visitor).

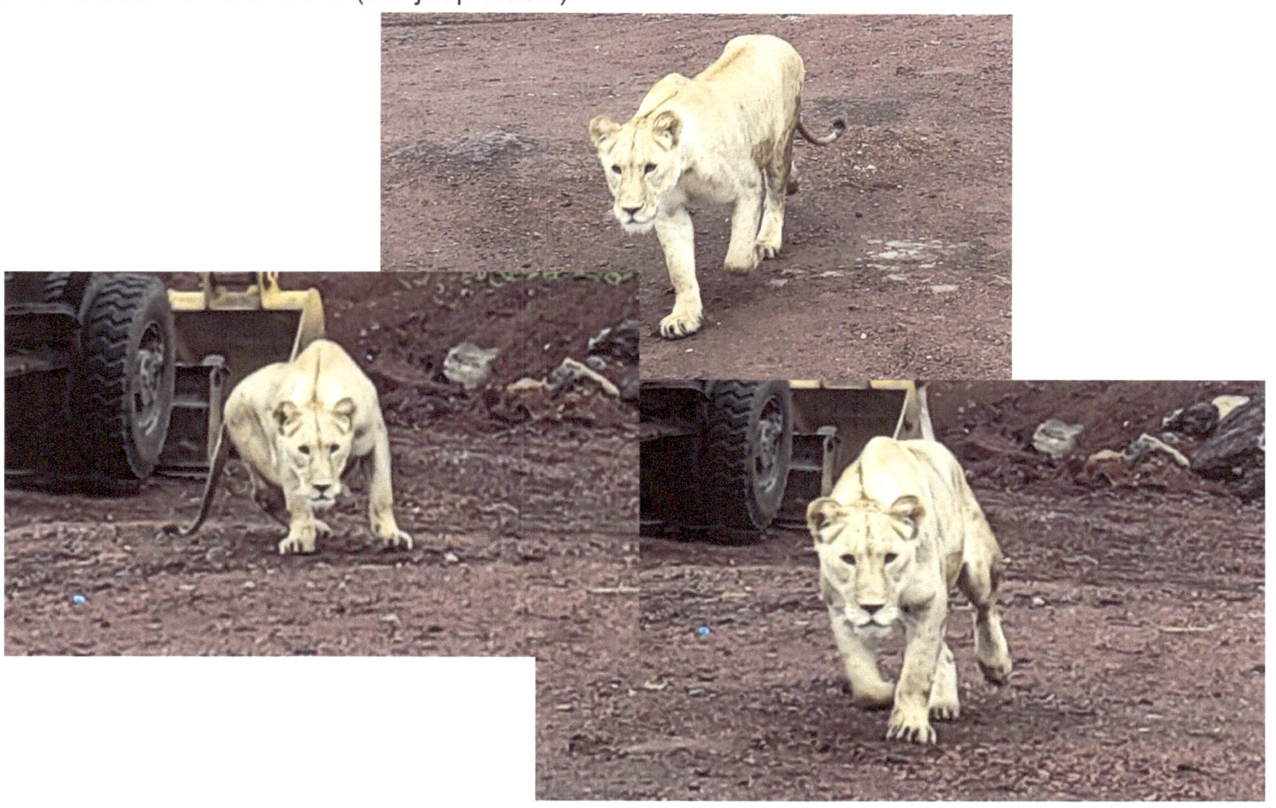

45

Farther away, more serious business was underway, morning mating time in Ngorongoro Crater. There is lots of resting until ready in between sessions, with apparently, and unsurprisingly, longer waits between times. She lets him know she's ready and waits until he is. And that makes 4 of the "Big Five". We learned that both genders get darker head coats / manes as they come of age.

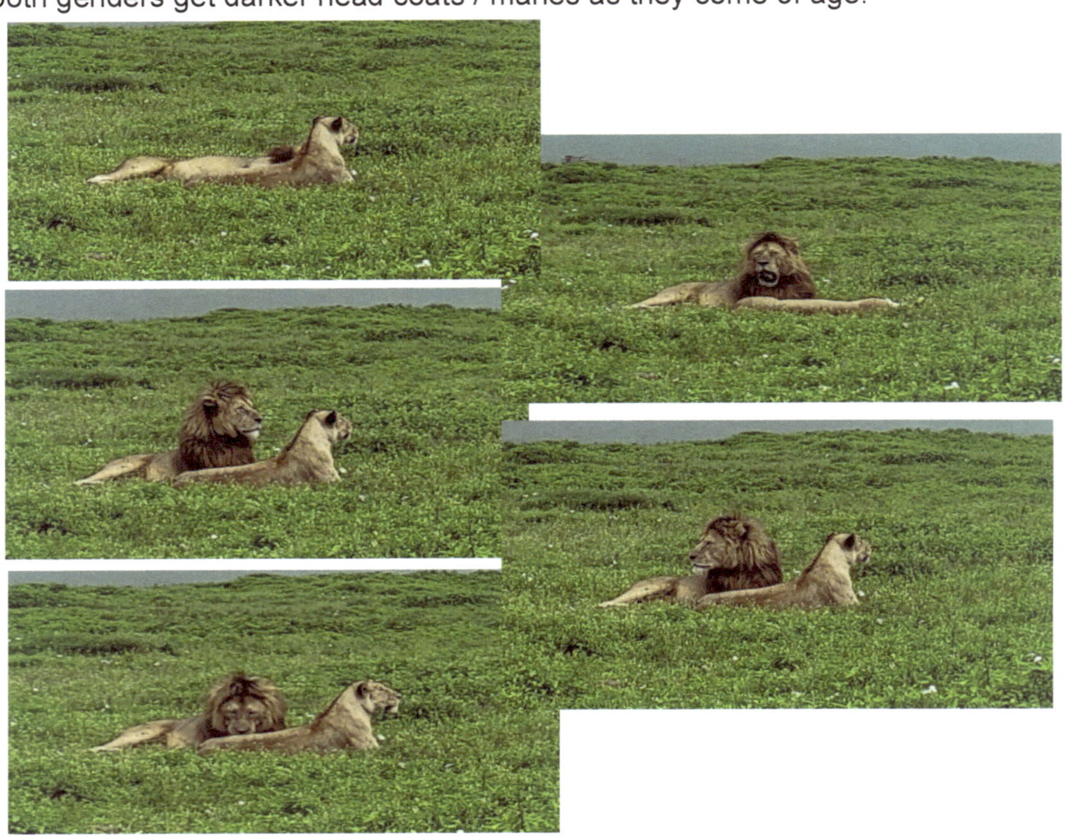

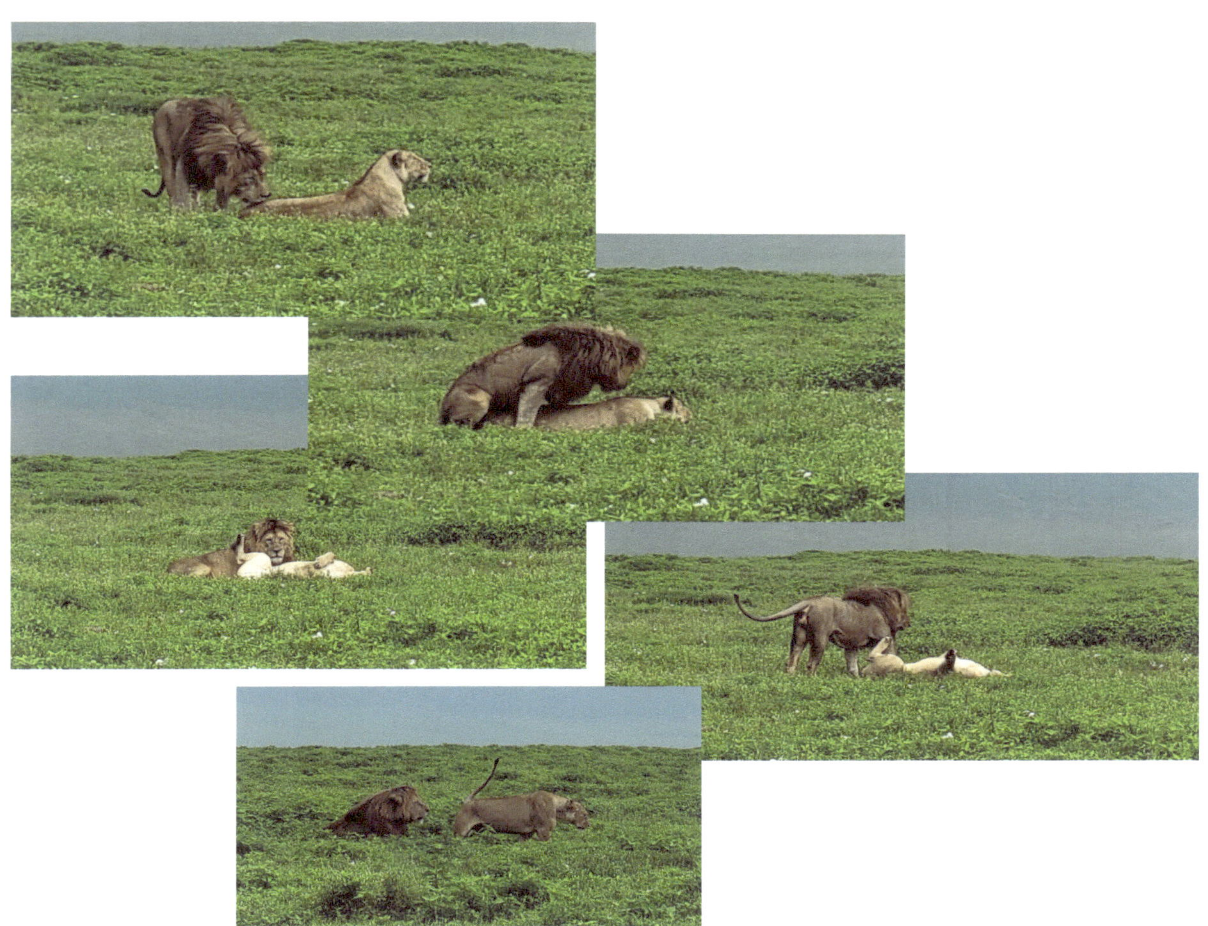

Ngorongoro hippos don't mind the alkaline water in Lake Magadi. One lone hippo, according to our guide, was probably taking a break after an encounter with another hippo, a timeout to relax and graze. The pile of rocks on the edge of the lake is really a "bloat" of hippos, perfectly named.

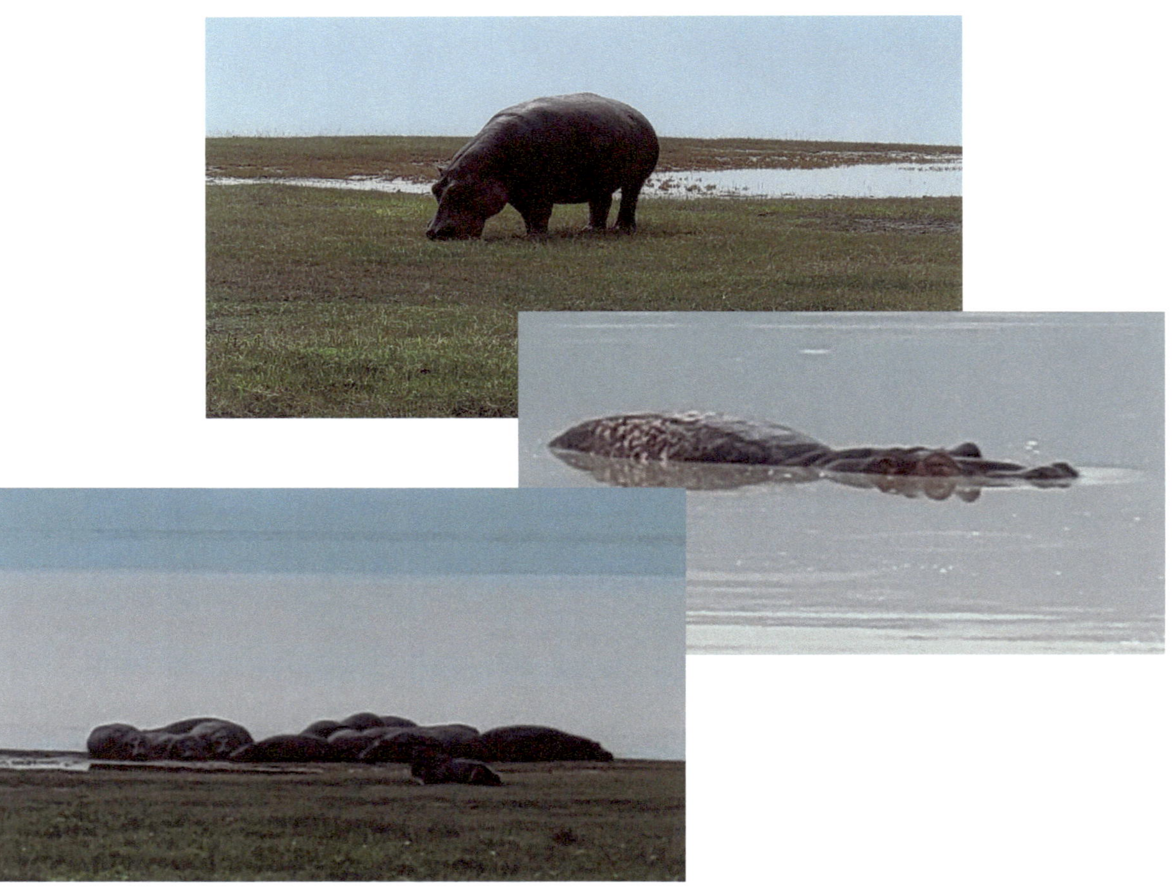

48

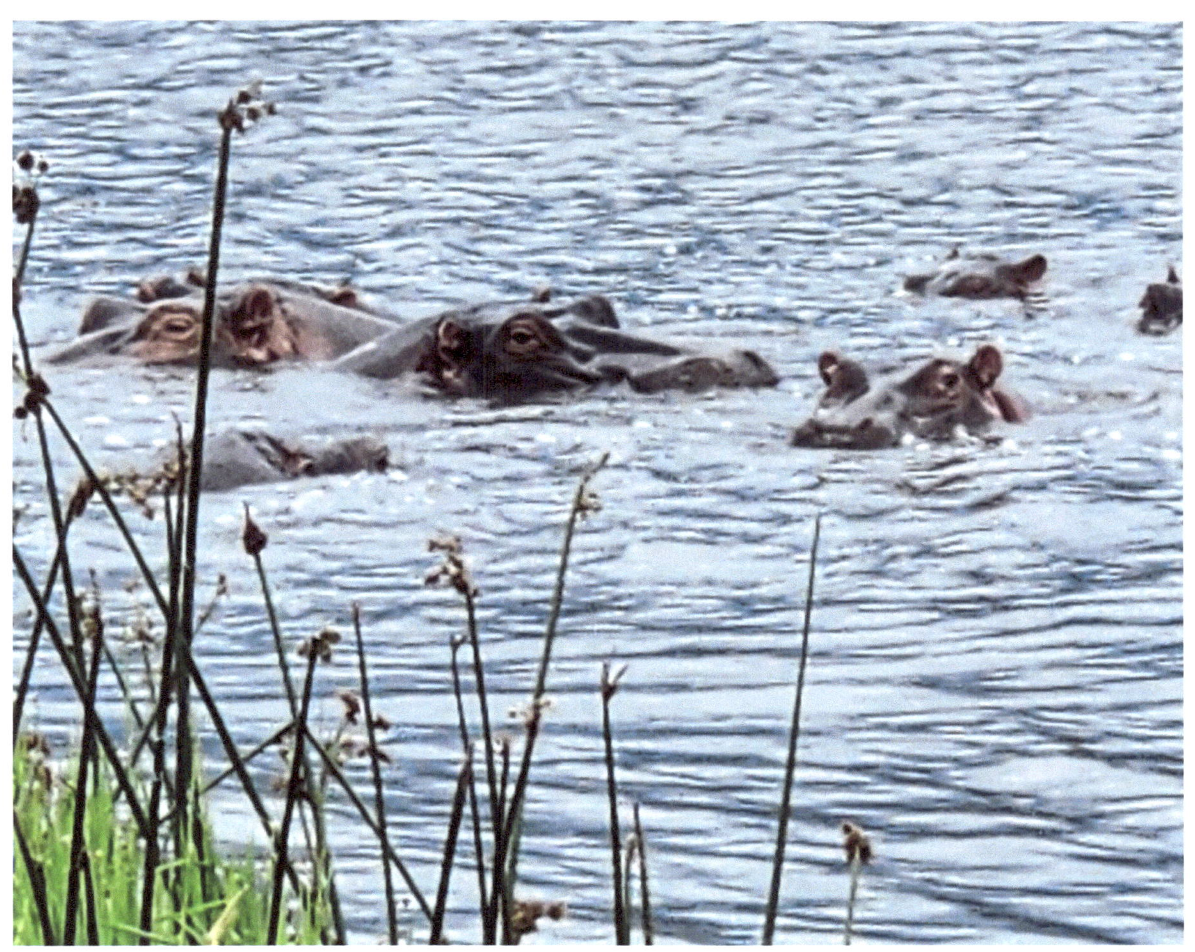

Our tour guide, with his high-powered camera lens, took a proper photo of the great mis-named Black Rhinoceros. I couldn't come close with my lame cell phone pic, ha ha. Some days go that way.

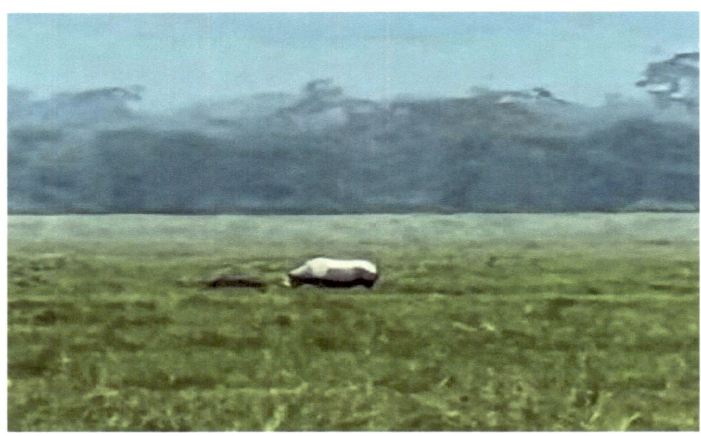

PS - Black Rhinos have extremely low-fat "black milk", so there's that, but they are misnamed because of the misnaming of the White Rhino, possibly a mis-interpretation of the Dutch label for "wide-mouth" rhinoceros (challenged theory). Oy!

"The story has a few variations but it basically states that the early Dutch settlers referred to this rhino as having a "wijde lip" or wide lip. The English mistook the word "wijde" (meaning wide) for "white" and so assumed that they were being called white rhinos by the Dutch."

In any case, the Black Rhino we saw in the Ngorongoro Conservation Area is endangered.
And that made our fourth of the big five animals of East Africa!

We were hoping at some point to see the elusive Leopard to make a full complement.

These Wildebeests are permanent residents at Ngorongoro Crater, according to our safari guide, not the famous migrating herds that were presently (in the Springtime) calving in the south.

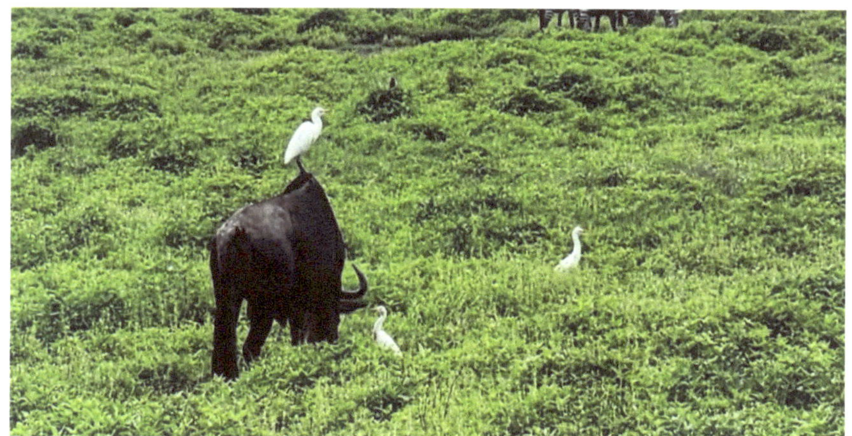

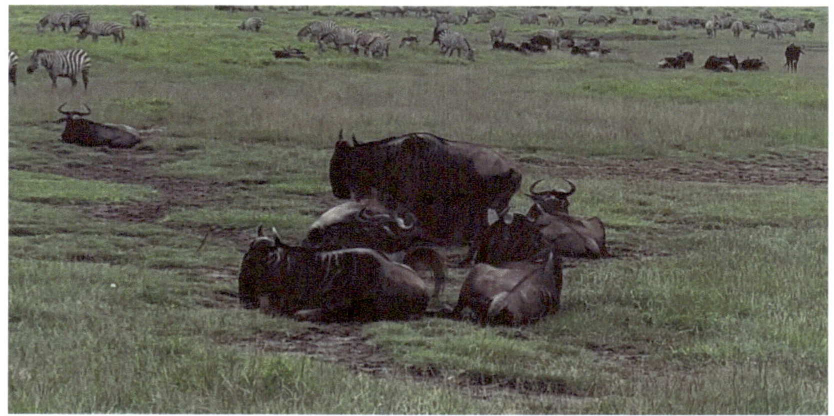

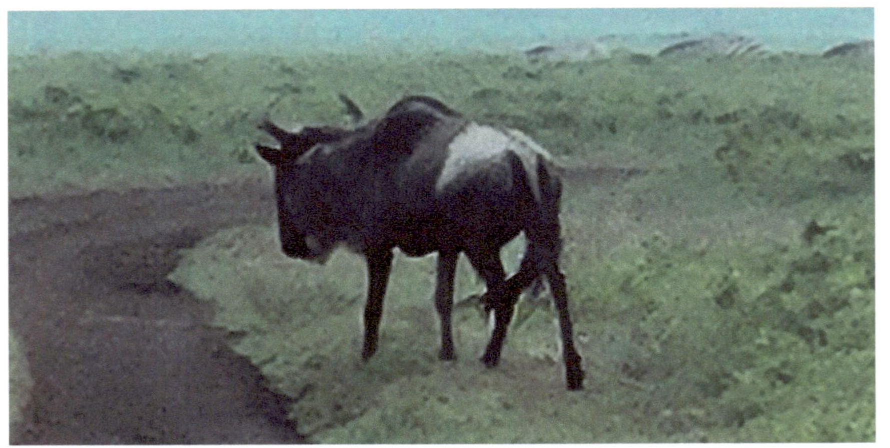

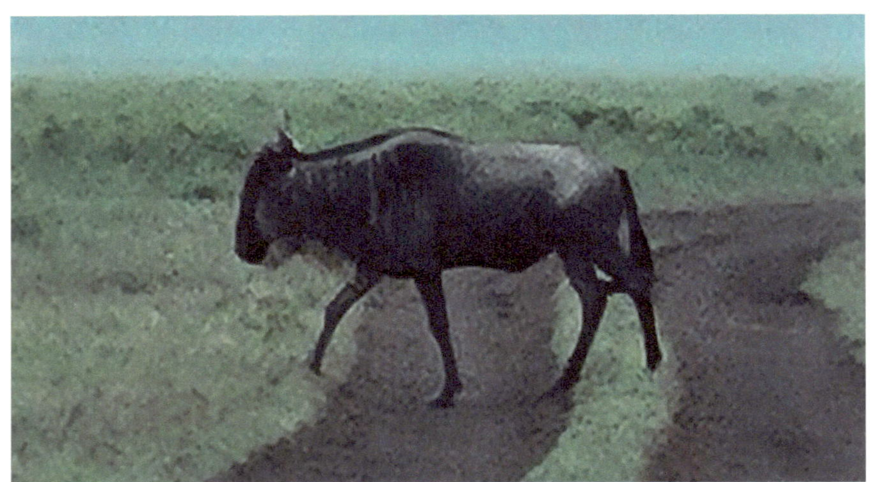

Lesser Flamingos, if I'm not mistaken. They live in Ngorongoro Caldera "Crater", feed in the alkaline water on spirulina grass (algae).

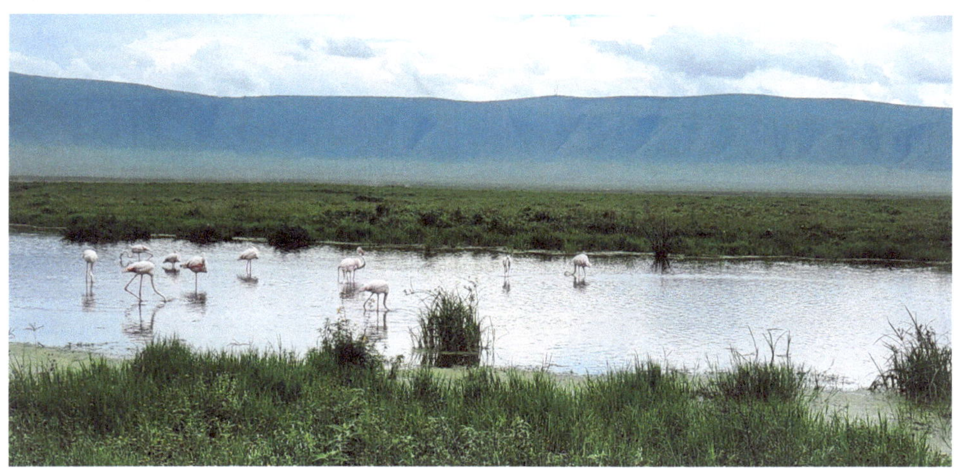

Lots of zebras and their foals are at Ngorongoro Crater in the Springtime (January). So sweet.

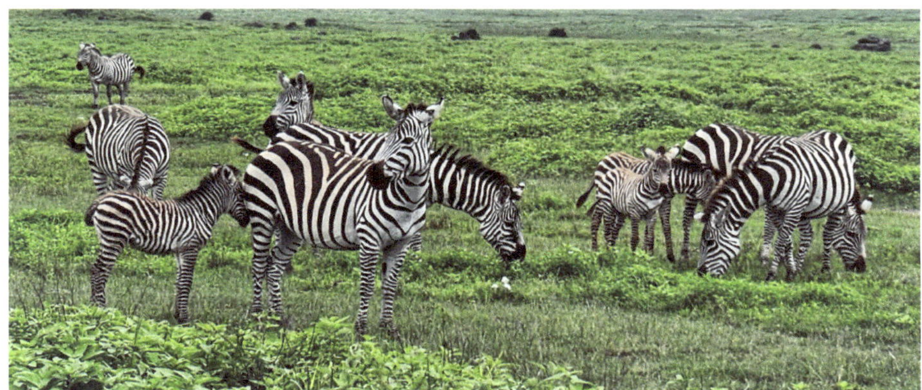

Ngorongoro Conservation Area, the Caldera / Crater has a large alkaline lake. No problem for these Buffalo Soldiers.

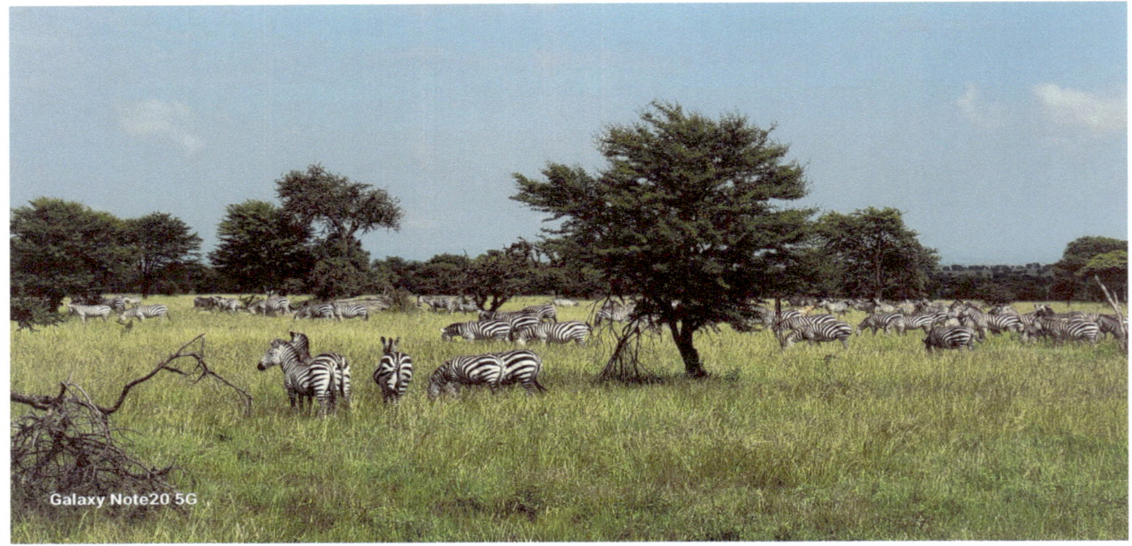

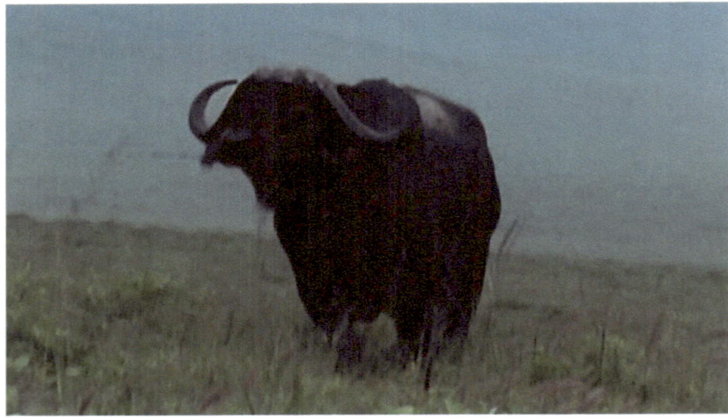

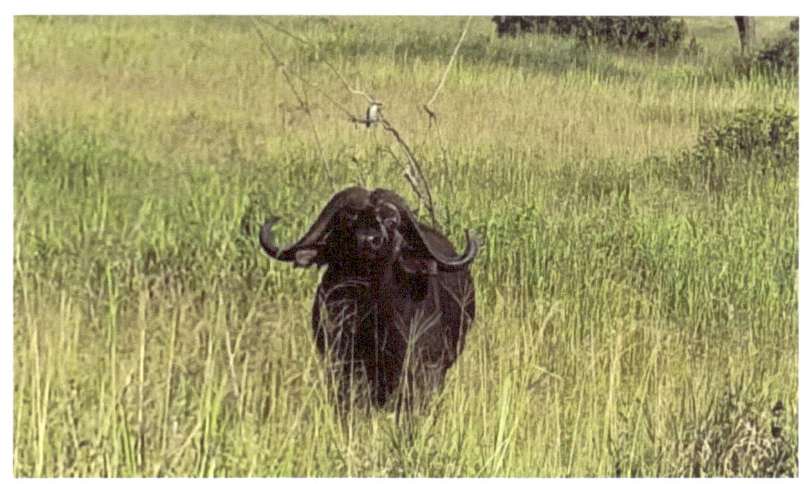

A "mixed herd" of Cape Buffaloes lives in the Ngorongoro Crater, including females, maybe a few calves.

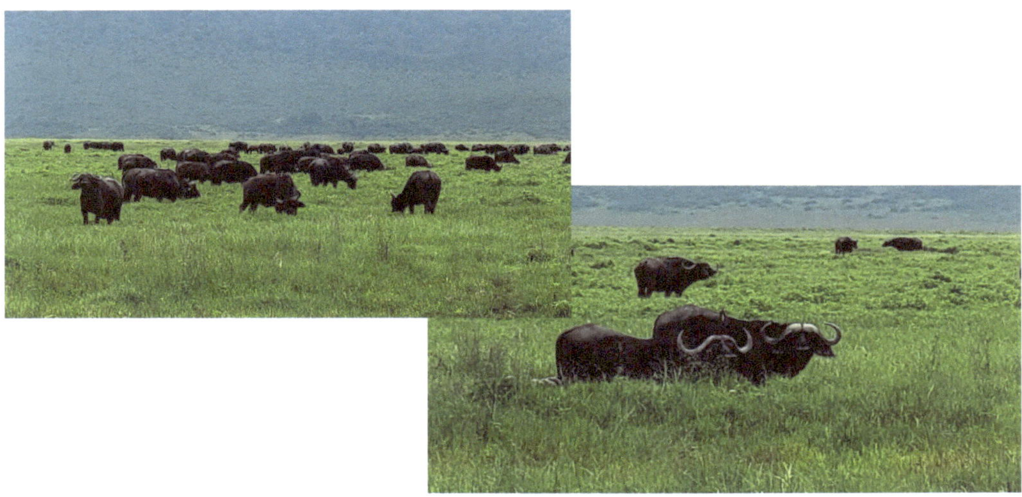

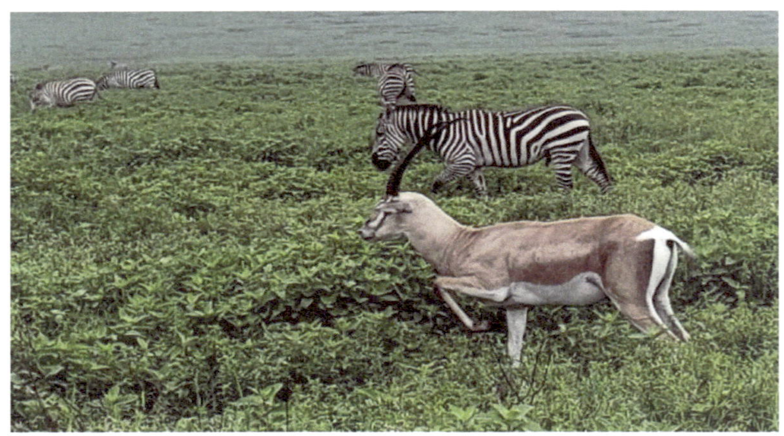

Grant's Gazelle and a zebra at Ngorongoro Crater.

Thompson "Tommy" Gazelle vs. Grant's Gazelle that has a white mustache above the tail. Tommies have the black side stripe.

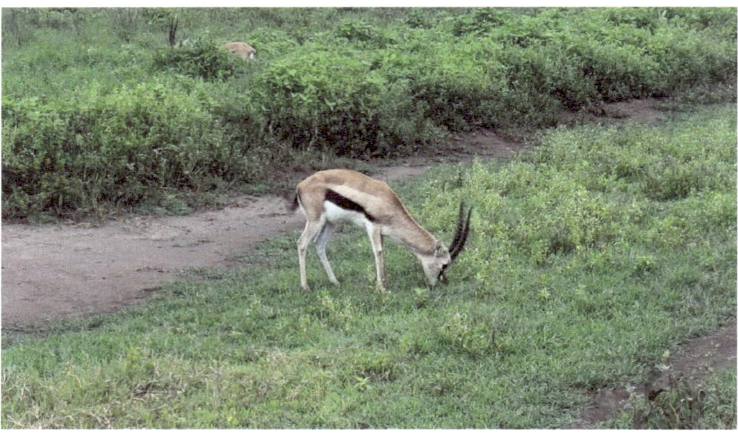

A view of Wildebeests running along Lake Magadi.

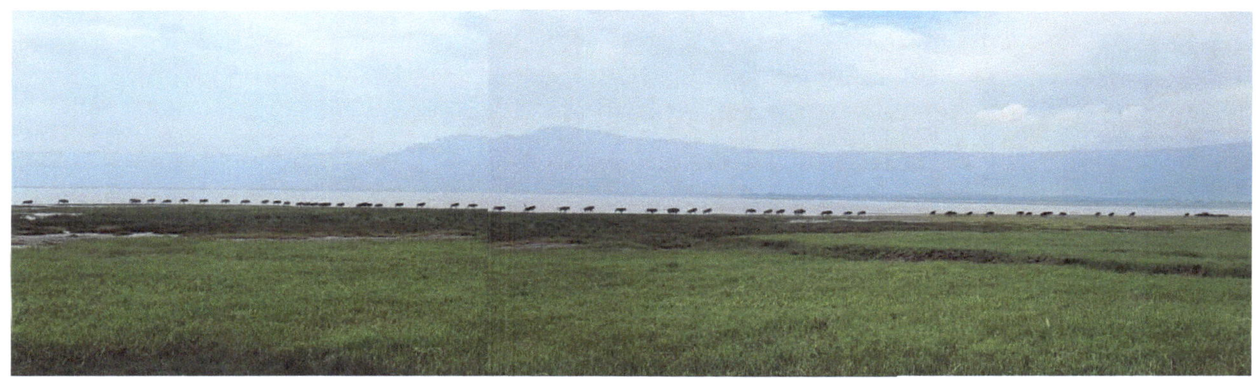

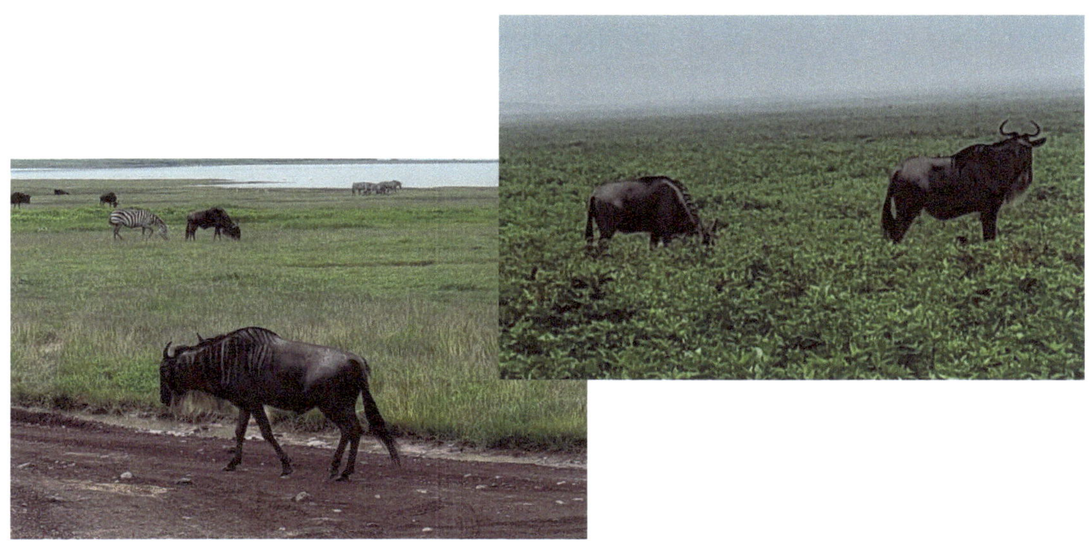

As we were moving along the roads of of the Ngorongoro Crater, I thought about the interpretive murals that we had seen painted on the wall around the pool at the Tarangire Safari Lodge, showing the "Small 5". Most of the safari tourism promos focus on the "Big 5" - a holdover from the days when tourism in Tanzania meant big game hunters after lions, elephants, rhinos, cape buffalo, and leopards. I loved this play on that and the reminder to keep my senses alert for all creatures great or small.

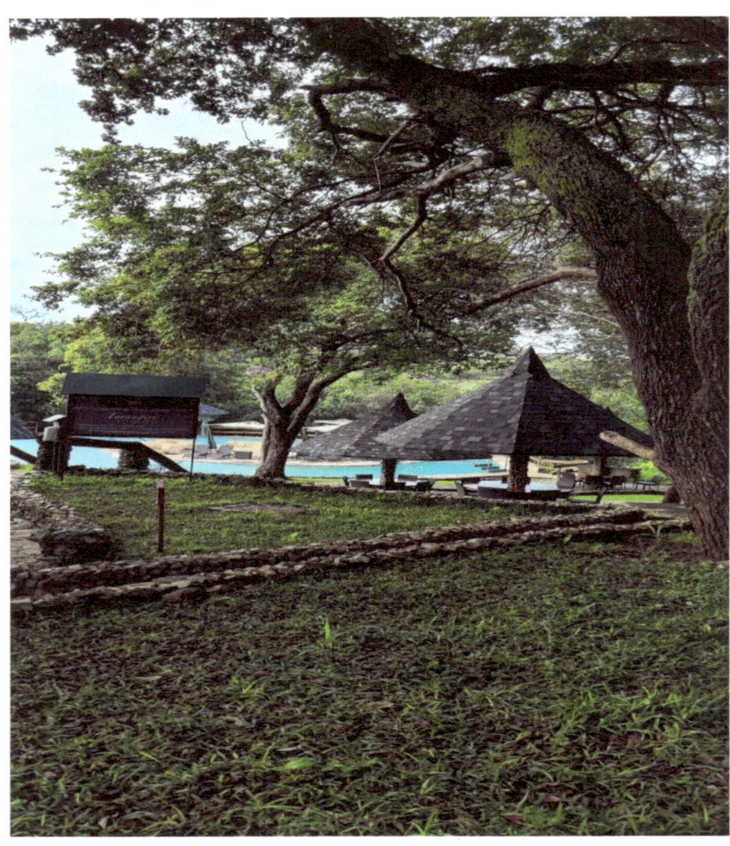

The CRATER in the...
...WET SEAS
(FROM LATE NOVEMBER TO MID MAY)
and in the...
...DRY SEAS
(FROM MID MAY TO LATE NOVEMBER)

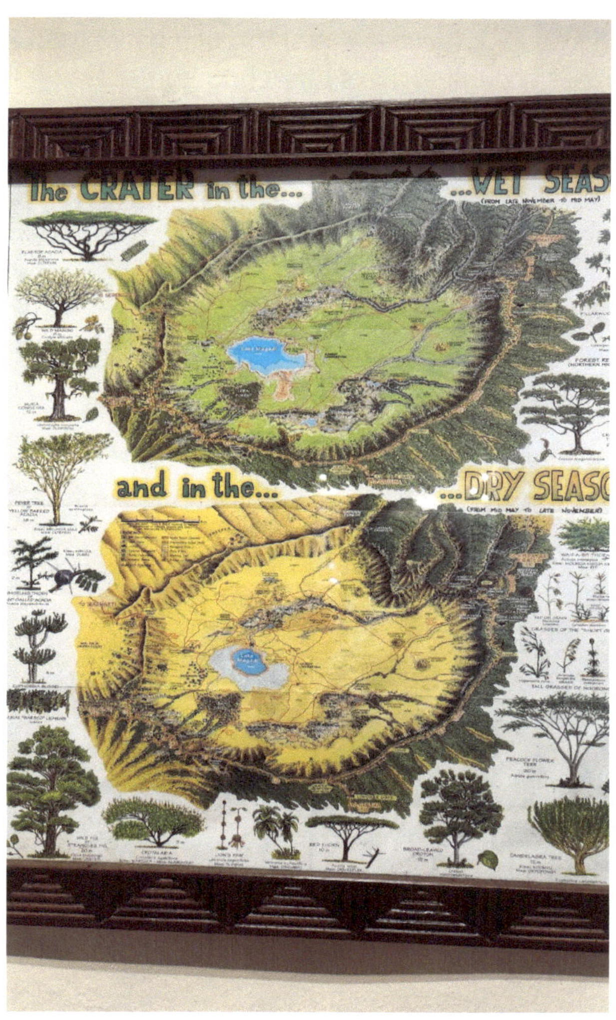

59

We left the Ngorongoro Crater Conservation Area and arrived near the south entrance of the Serengeti. There is an impressive interpretive center just as you are approaching Serengeti, providing information about early human evolution and development, paleoanthropology, in the Olduvai Gorge national park entrance, acknowledging the breakthrough work of Mary and Louis Leaky

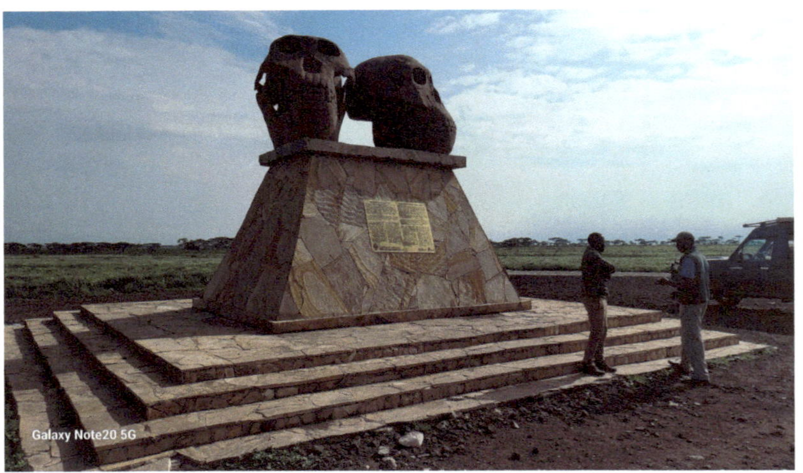

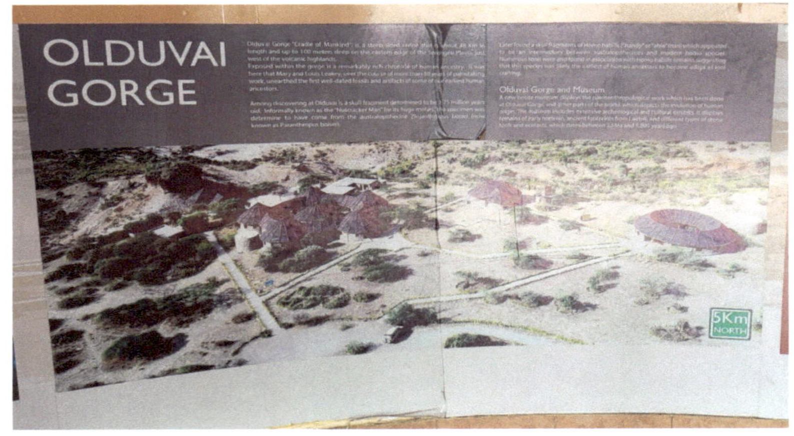

The blue image below, is a footprint from 3.5 million years ago, showing upright walking, bipedalism, of human ancestors.

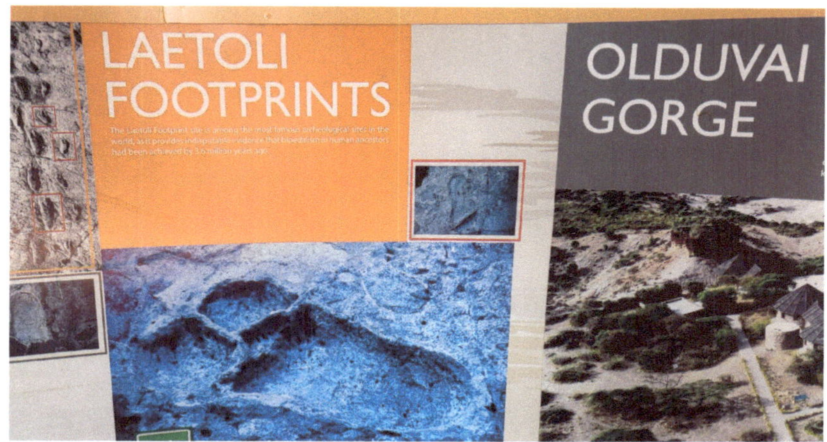

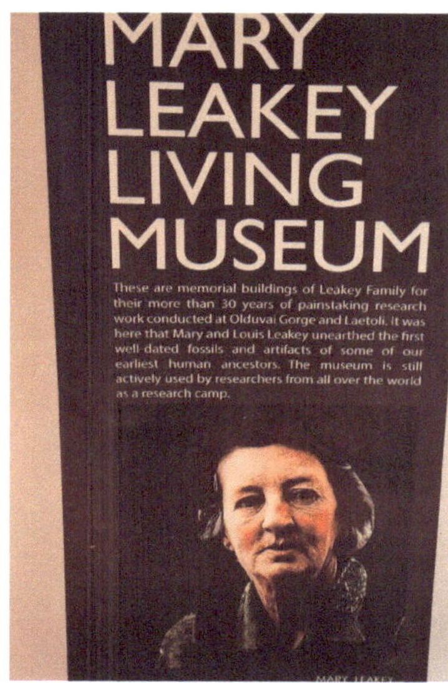

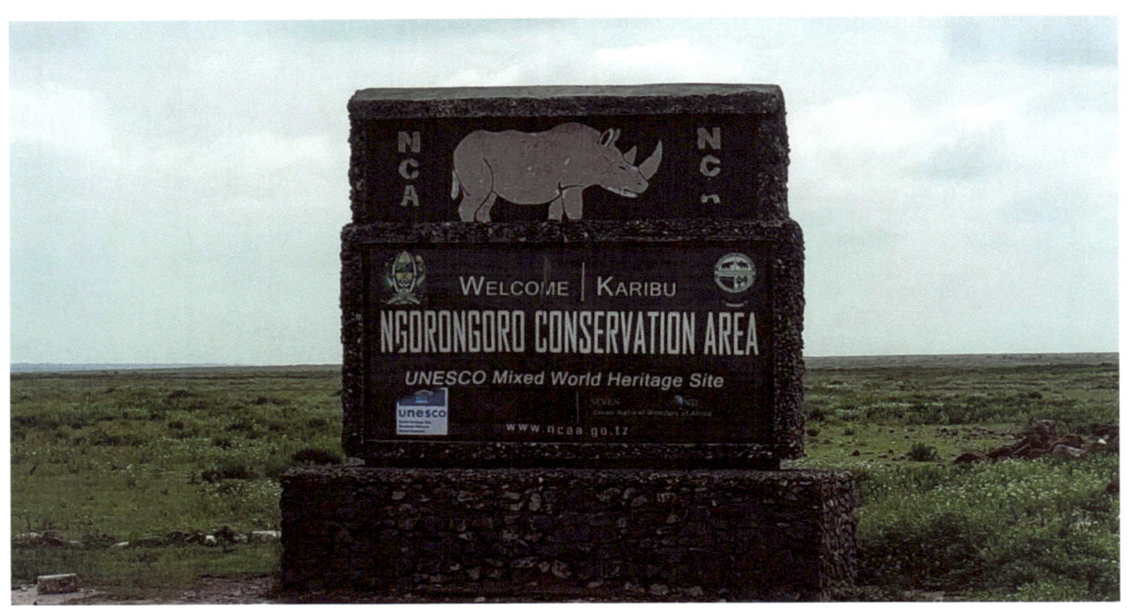

NCA
NCA
WELCOME | KARIBU
NGORONGORO CONSERVATION AREA
UNESCO Mixed World Heritage Site
unesco
www.ncaa.go.tz

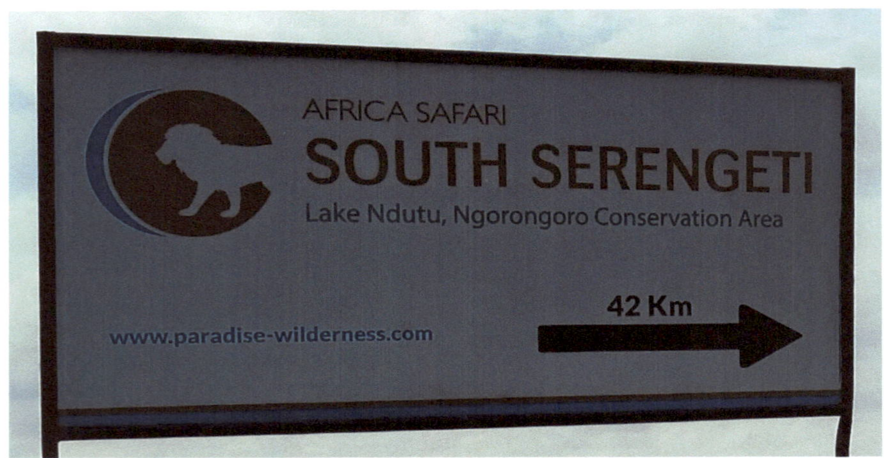

AFRICA SAFARI
SOUTH SERENGETI
Lake Ndutu, Ngorongoro Conservation Area
www.paradise-wilderness.com
42 Km

We made it to the entrance (not the gate) of the Serengeti after passing a lion with her darling cubs, trying to get away from bothersome flies. They ended up going down into the road culvert to wait them out. And we took off, also being harassed by the same flies - none of which were at the lovely entrance.

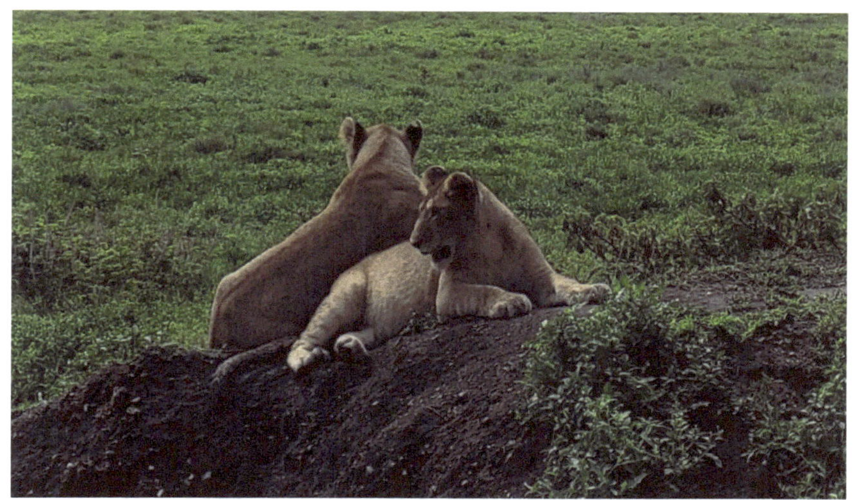

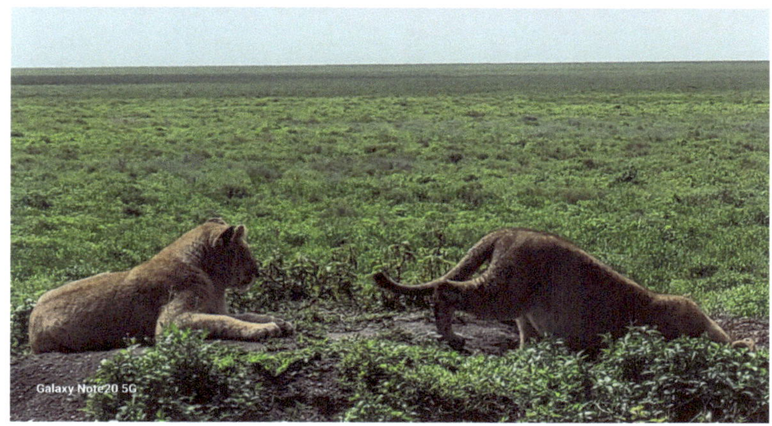

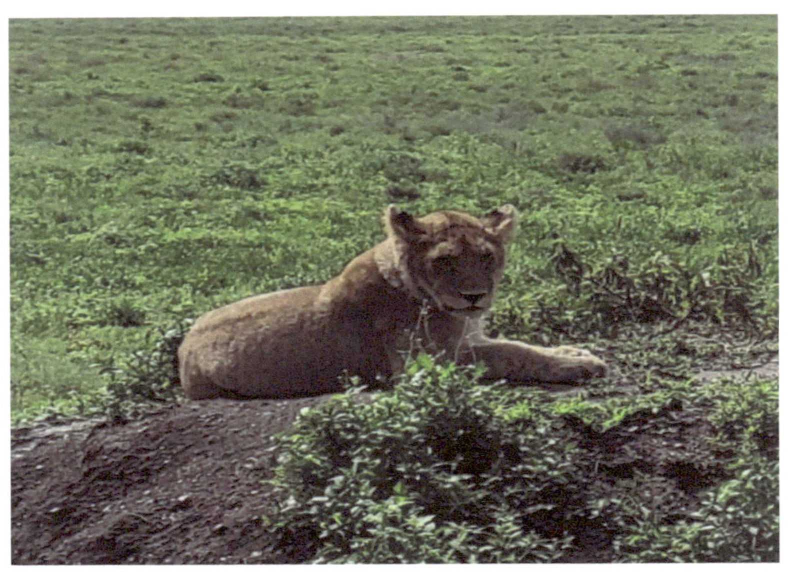

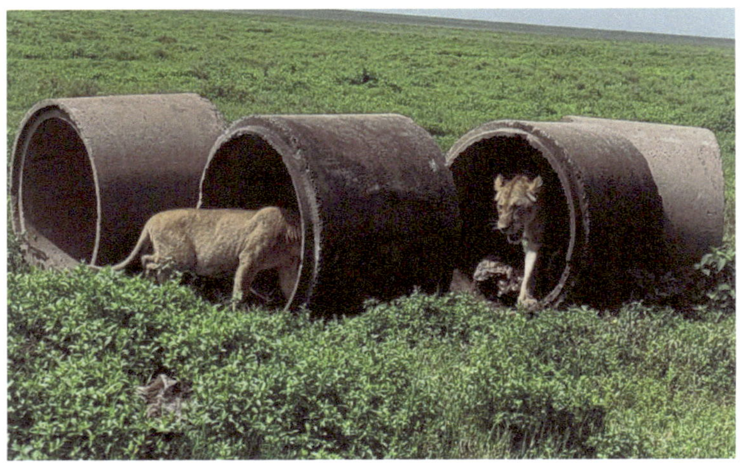

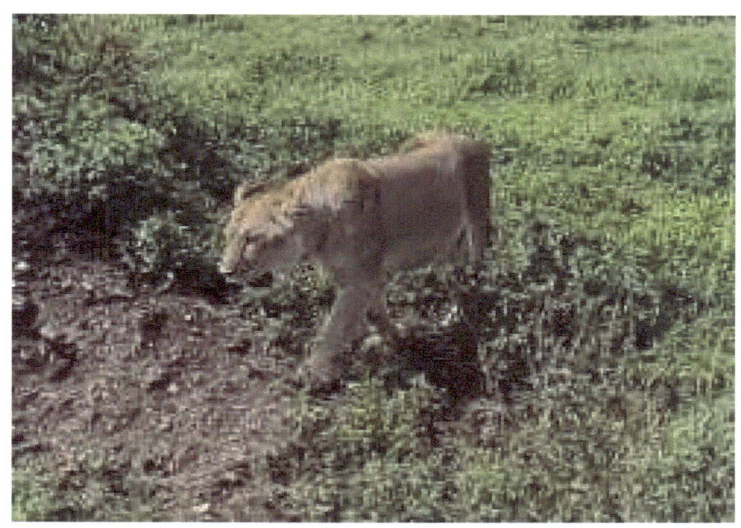

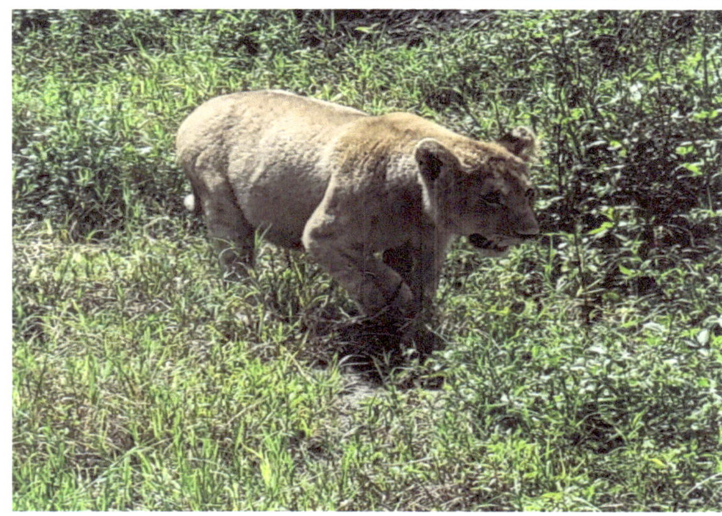

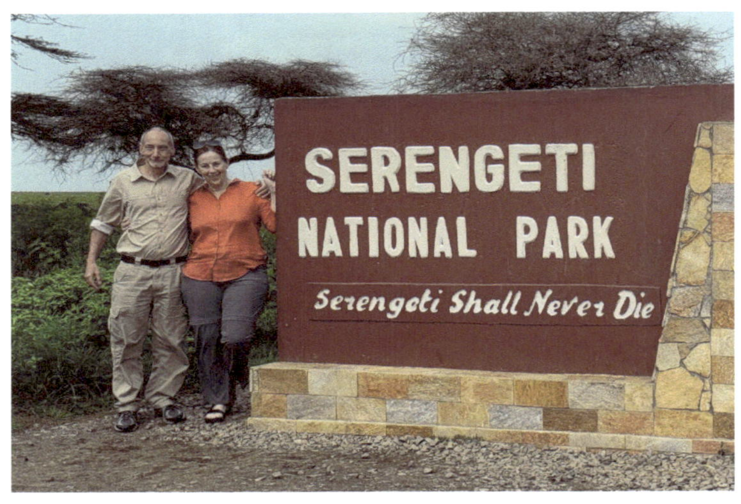

SERENGETI
NATIONAL PARK
Serengeti Shall Never Die

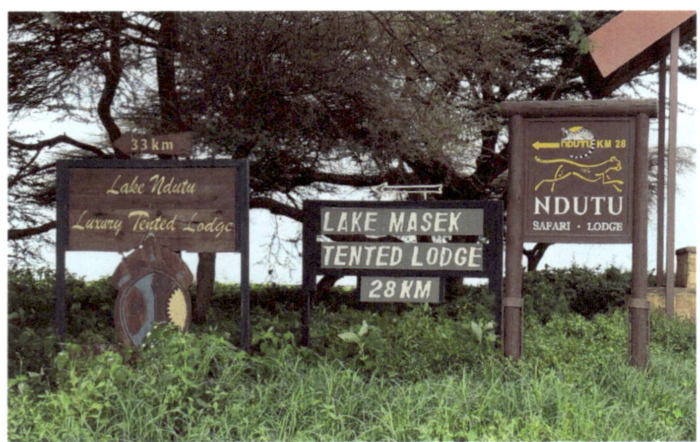

33 km
Lake Ndutu
Luxury Tented Lodge
LAKE MASEK
TENTED LODGE
28 KM
NDUTU KM 28
NDUTU
SAFARI · LODGE

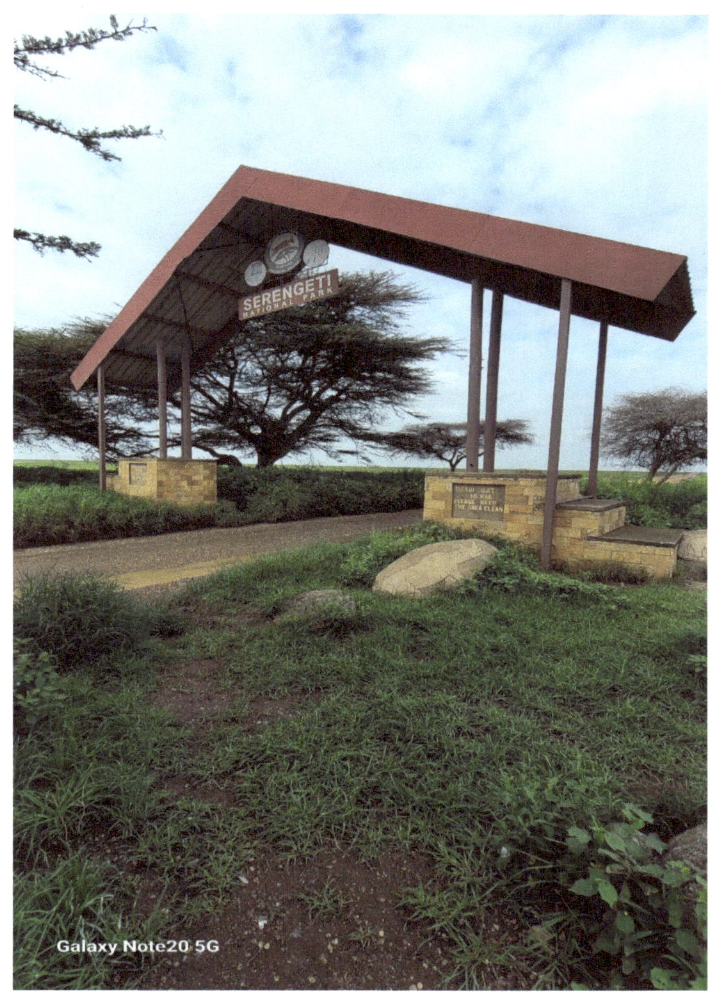
SERENGETI
NATIONAL PARK

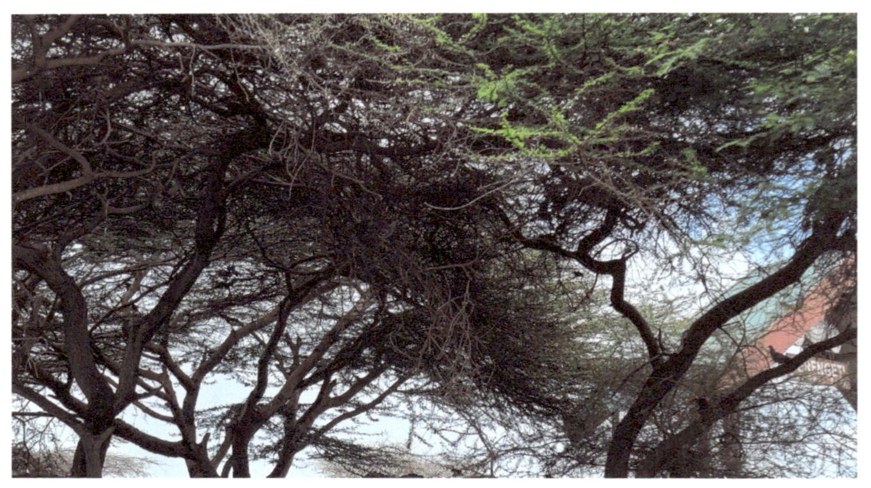

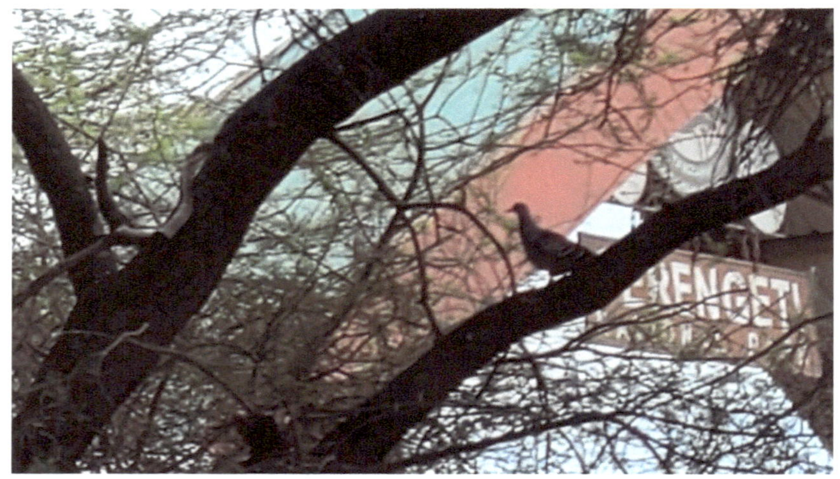
ERENGETI

Hyenas m,

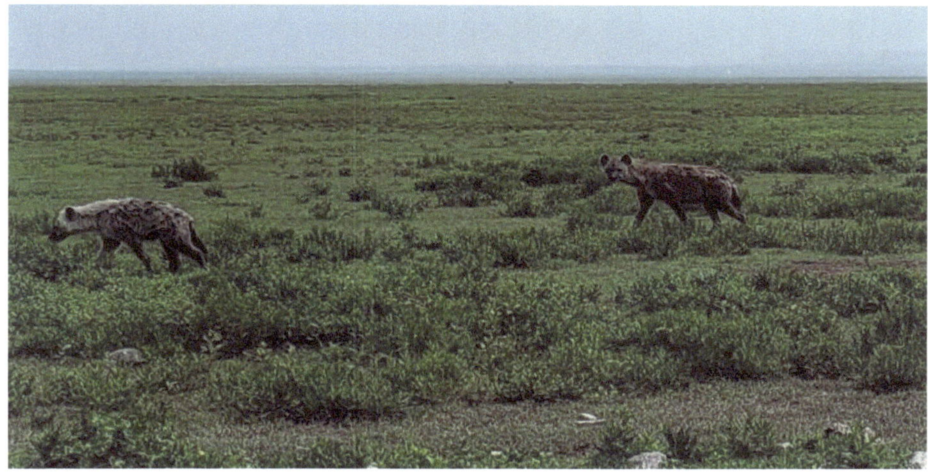

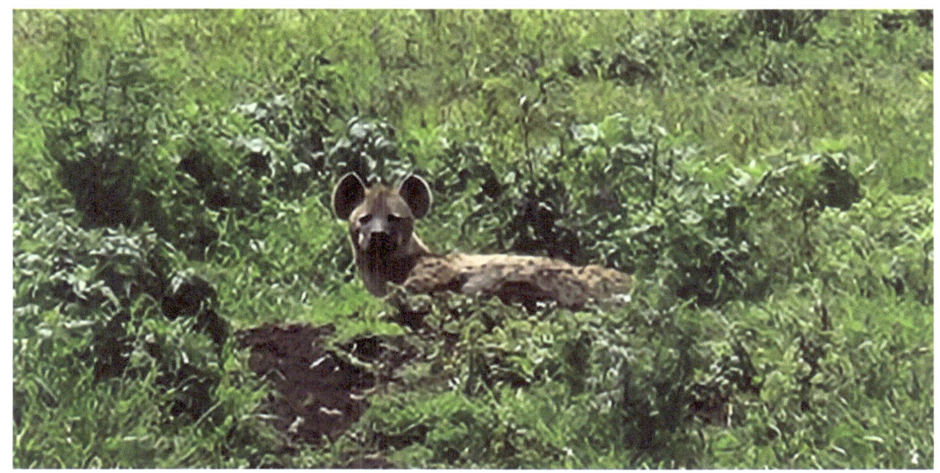

Pumbas (warthogs) – "Hakuna matata!" Locals say that (meaning "no worries") all the time, at least to tourists.

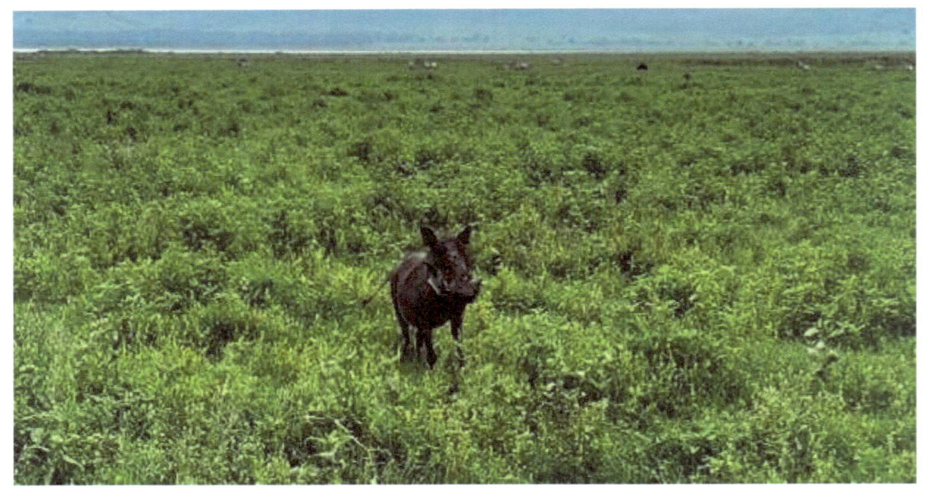

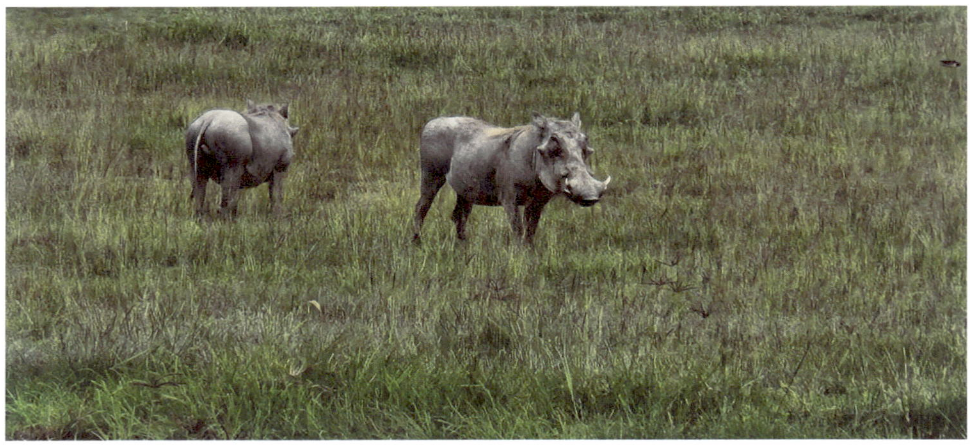

The Serengeti South Gate

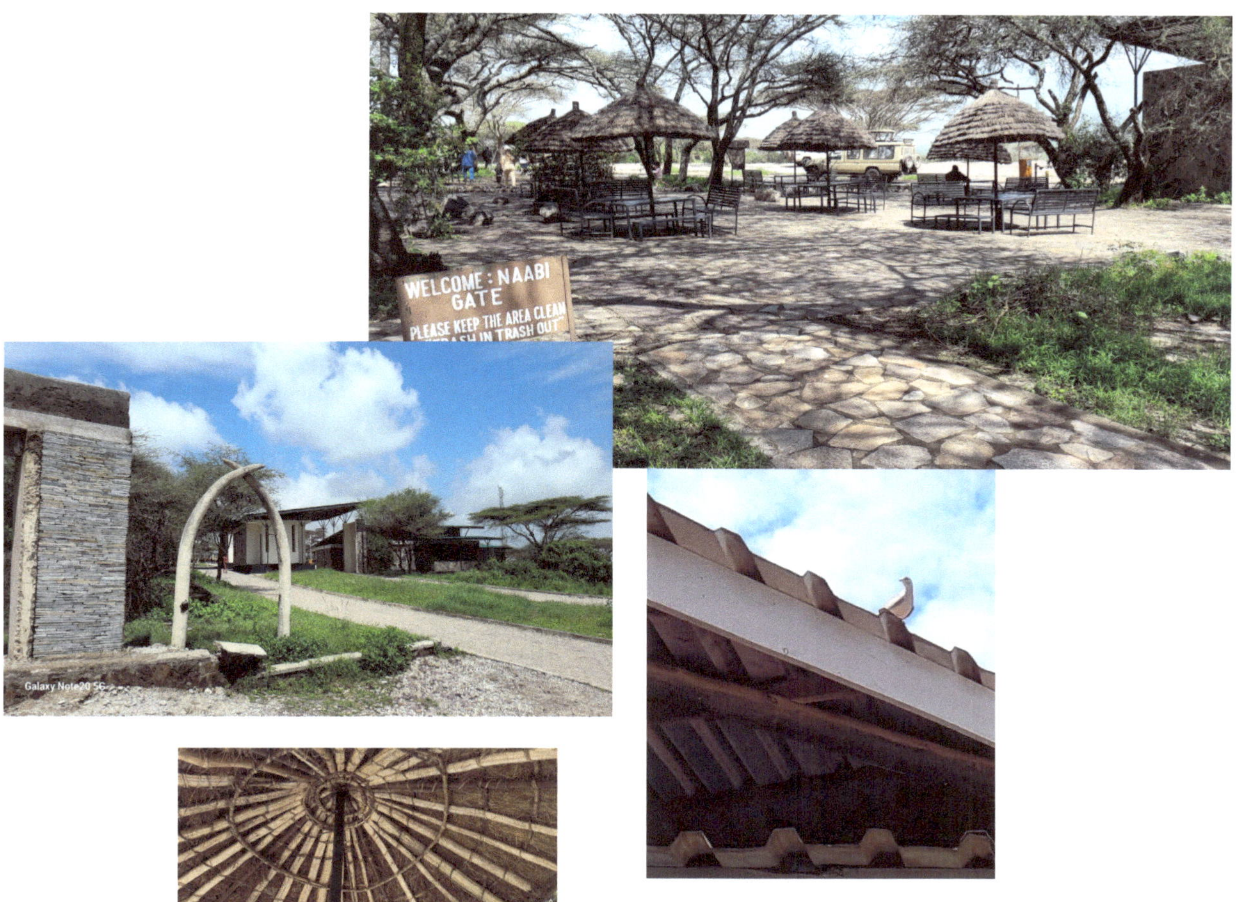

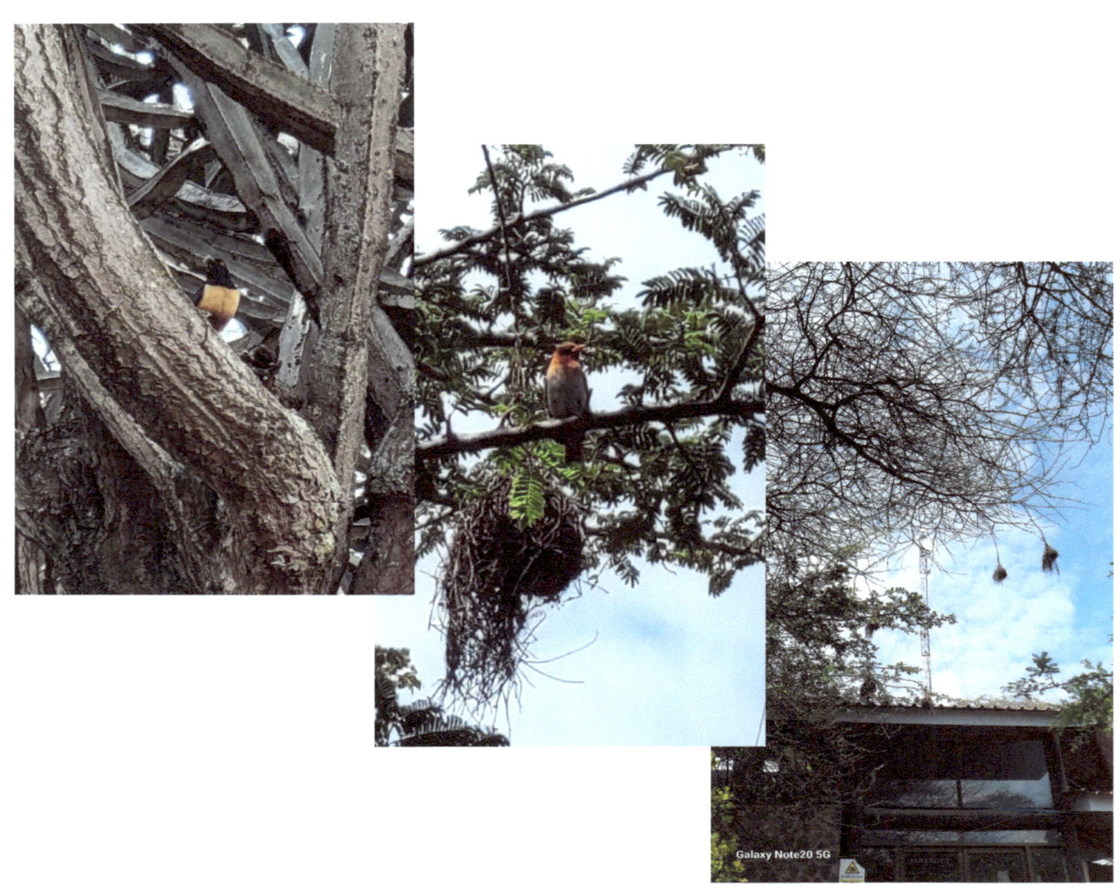

Galaxy Note20 5G

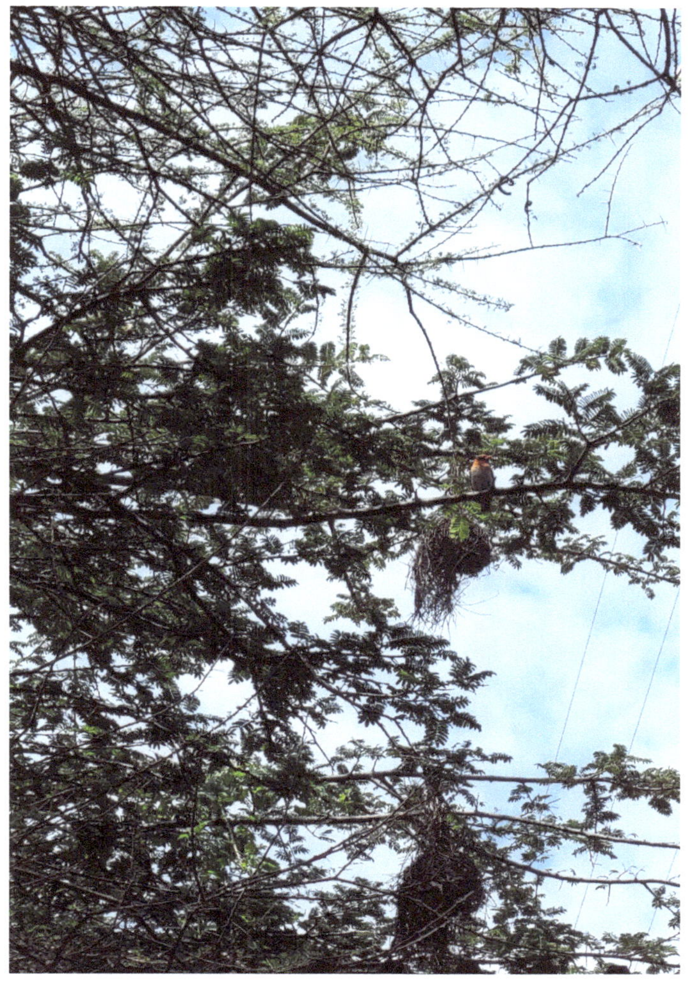

Ndutu, Central Serengeti .... and lunch.

We ate next to a nearly mature male, 4-4.5 year-old boy who was chuffing to call his 3 brothers, panting heavy, probably after a big feast during the night before. He was totally uninterested in us.

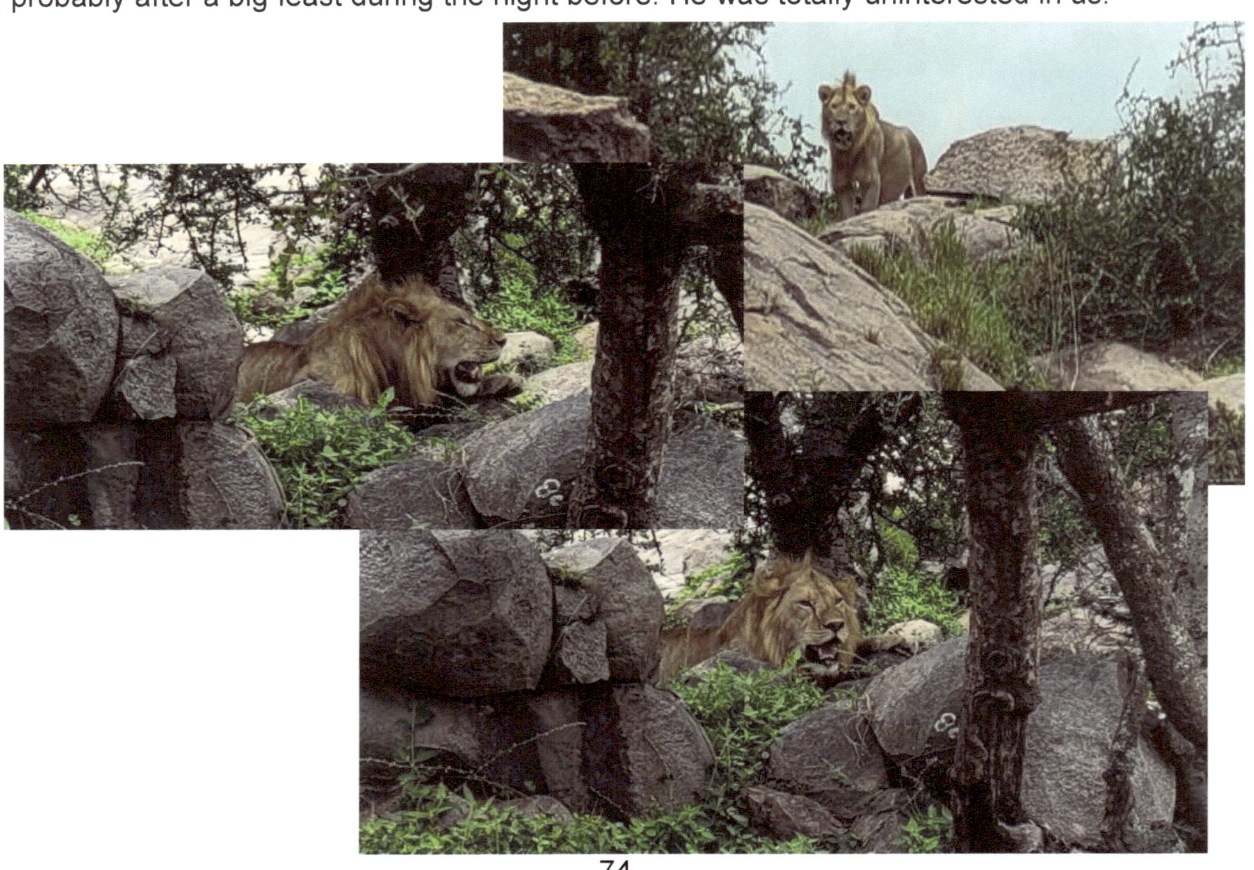

We hung out among four brothers (mostly one, and one brother who passed by). Just us, and the lions. #boysclub

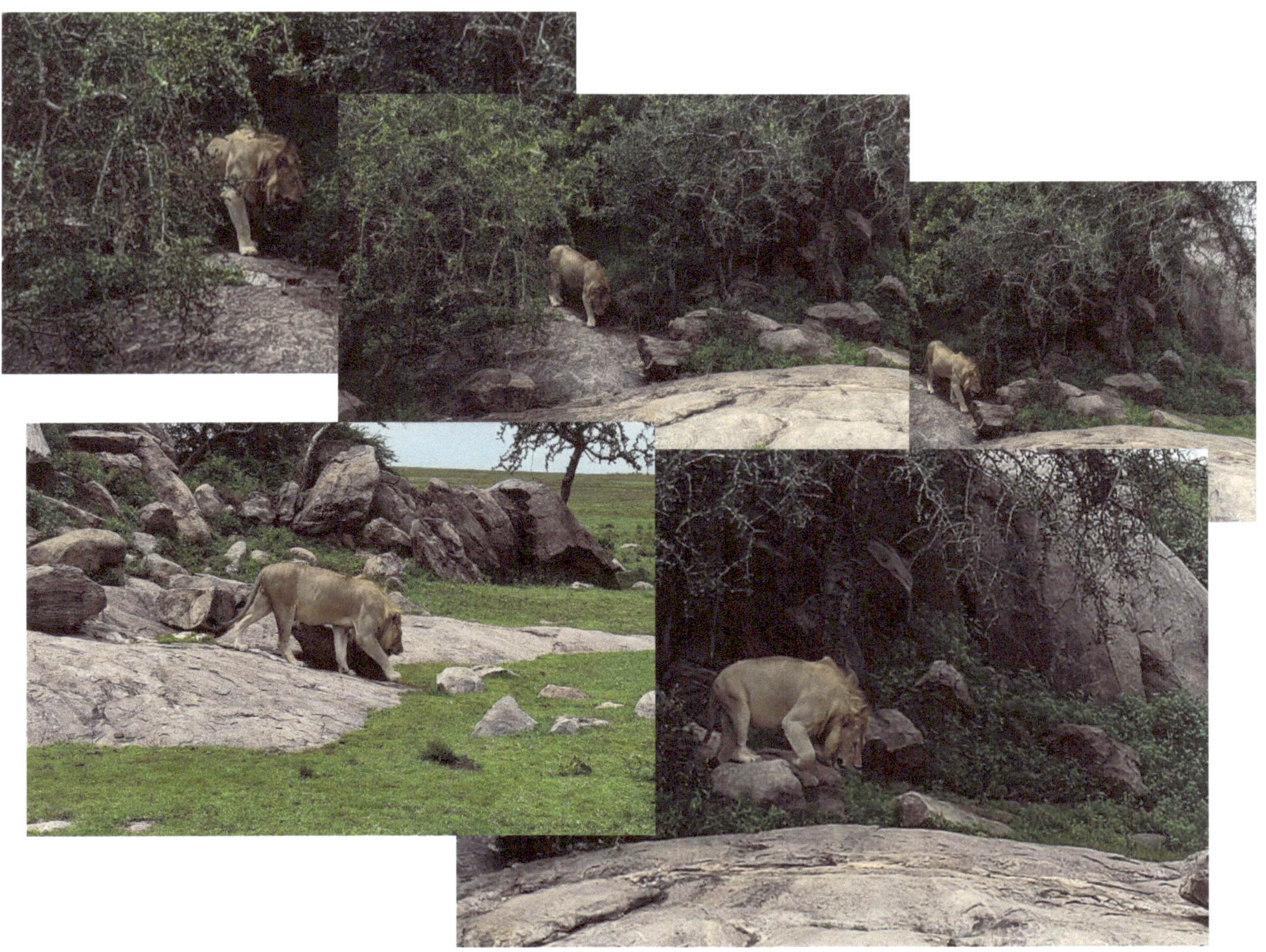

75

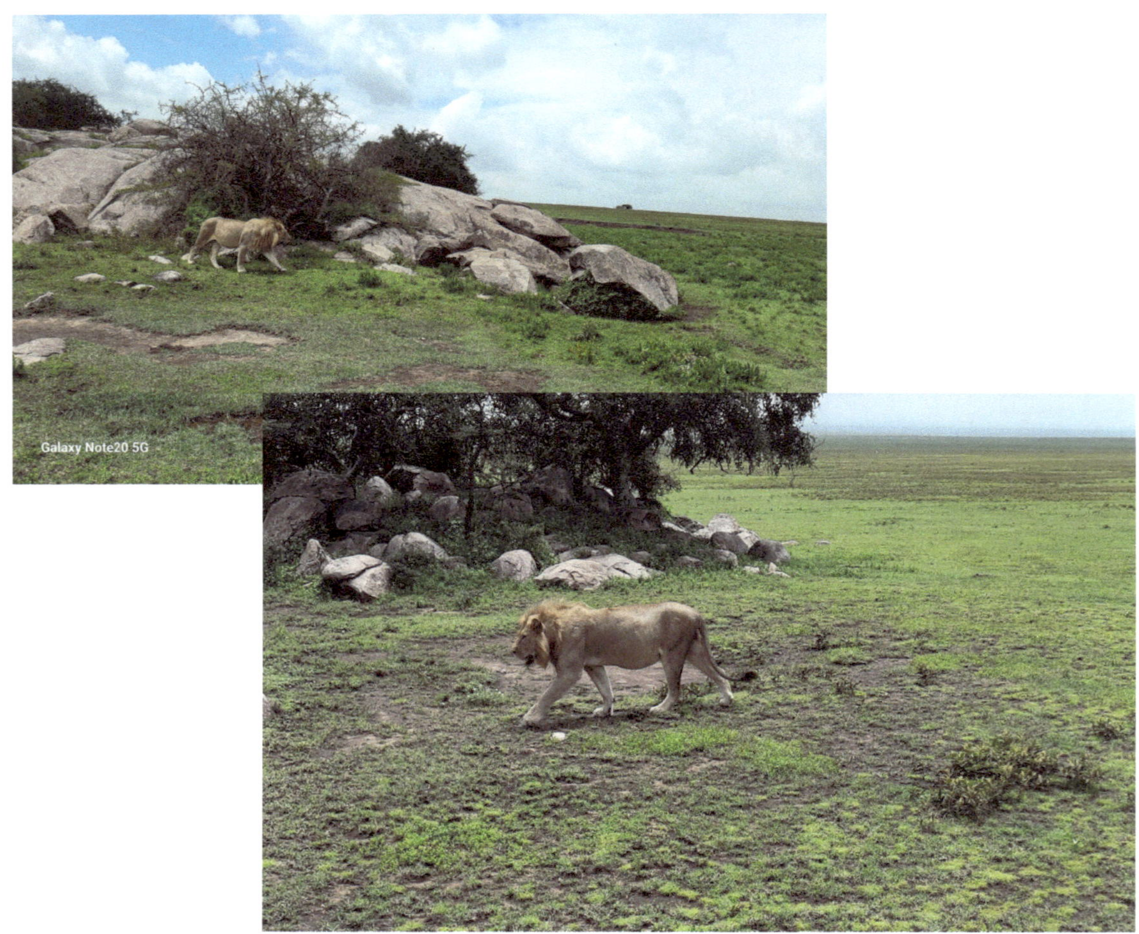

After lunch next to a lion, the guys had to, "check the tires" ("take a leak"). I decided they were mad (insane). Somehow it worked out fine. The easiness was short-lived.

See our guide on the passenger's side, left side of the vehicle? And the lion away up on the hill? That's because our plan to leave was foiled by a single soft mud spot behind the back right tire - we were deeply stuck. Our guide got out and shooshed the lion away, "Go on, get out of here", and a fake throwing of something (very Maasai lion hunter style, (he's not Maasai), just used the gesture that the lions know). Big Boy took off, looking confused to be interrupted from his nice nap. But he never left our sight. And his brother joined him on the ridge for a bit. One trailed off, i. e., the other Big Boy cut a wide berth and circled on the ridge, intending to get back to his happy den of rocks. Oh, and there were rain clouds headed our way.

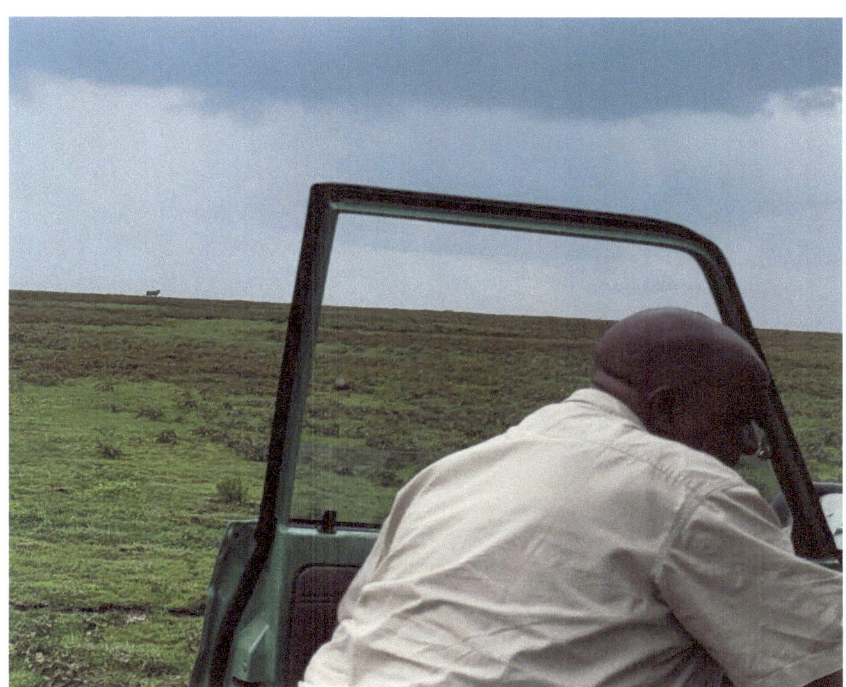

With Big Boy up on the ridge and pending rain, the guys decide they needed rocks from the lions' home to lift our stuck tire out of the mud, so they formed a plan to take the two tire covers, one for beating with a crow bar to make disturbing noise, and one for hauling back rocks to put under the jacked-up tire. They also concluded they needed to pull out the jeep floormat, as Zach called it "a geo textile solution" layer to add on top. 😁 I had full confidence in our cadre of experienced brave men.

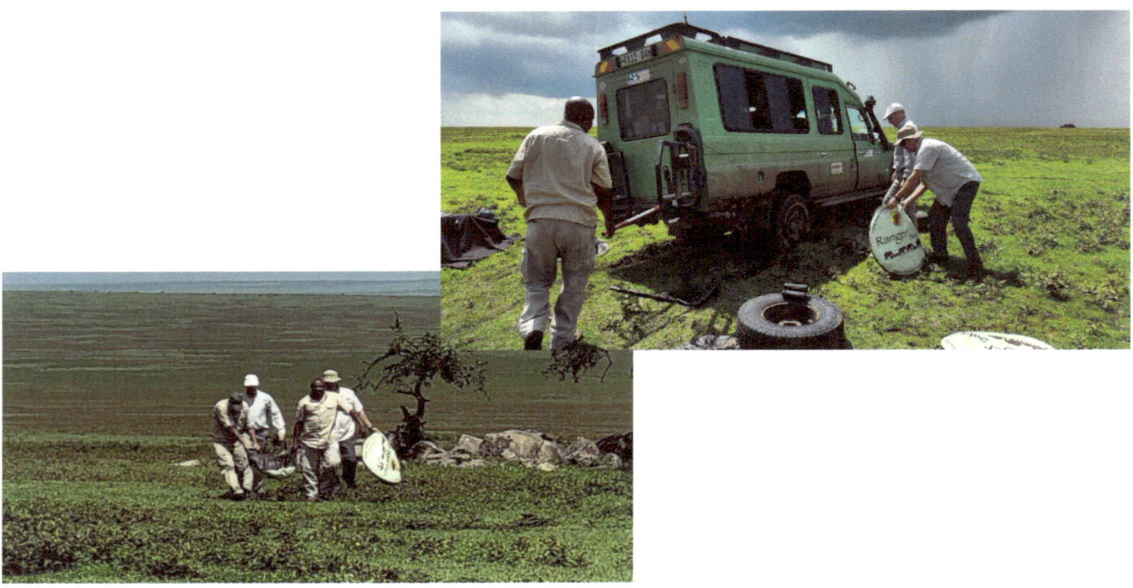

After hearing one crazy story where a woman and her children got out of the jeep, so they wouldn't be left behind after dark, and followed the husband and driver to get help, only to encounter angry elephants and barely make it out alive, I concluded to my female travel mates that the lesson learned there is "this woman is staying in the jeep". That worked because we spent our time lion-spotting, reporting their whereabouts, and photographing the event. All good. …. Look at that rain in the distance where we were headed.

The jeep was backed out of the mud, we picked up the broken jack and shovel, made one pass around an adjacent rock outcrop where we spotted the two other brothers having a siesta on top, then high-tailed it on the high roads - because the guide knew not to dare go down to the 2 low
roads where, we later learned, 3 jeeps with 18 people headed to our camp ended up spending the night - stuck in the mud.

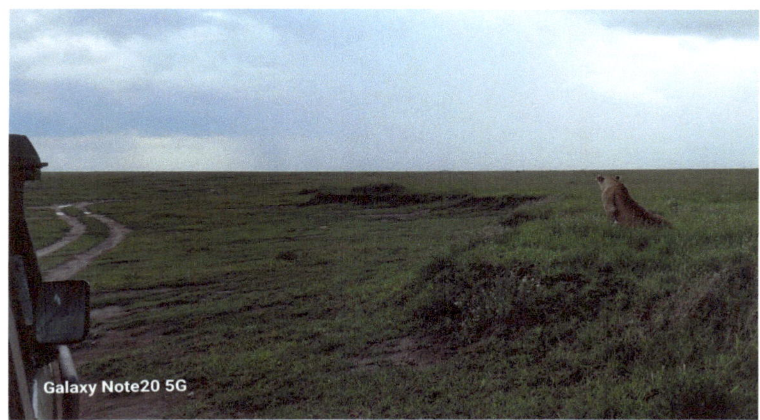

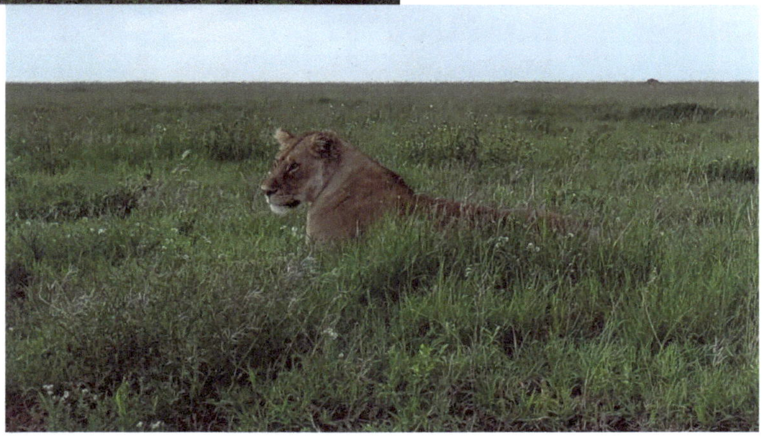

Once on the road, and wanting to avoid at all costs getting stuck again, we raced through pouring rain, fogged up windows and bumps that shortened our spines and rattled our teeth and brains; tightened seat belts pulled us back down to the seats after every major bump. We broke out into sunlight once again and resumed our safari search once again. Soon, our guide noticed we had disturbed a leopard stalking this Topi Antelope.

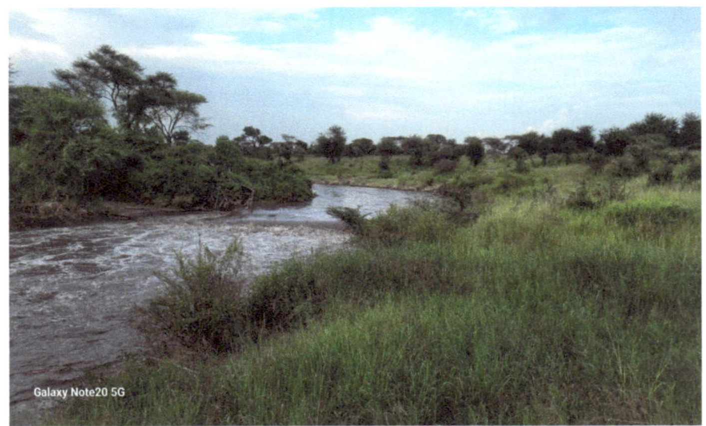

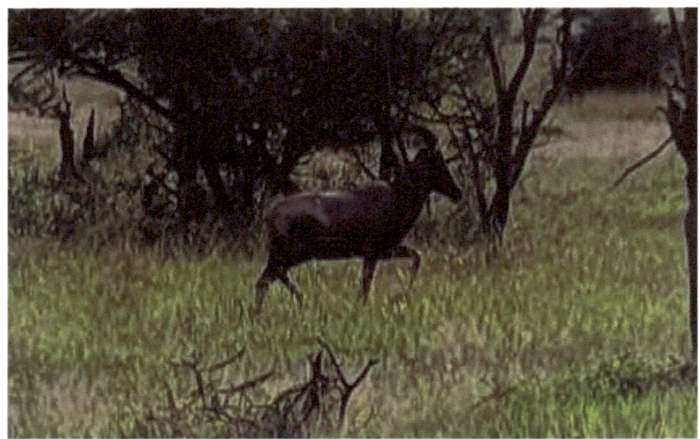

We could hardly follow the leopard slinking away through the grass - except for that white tail tip that flipped up occasionally - designed so cubs can follow. Maybe it was a female. 🖤 🤍 🖤

And that is number 5, of the "Big Five"! (Elephant, Cape Buffalo, Lion, Black Rhino and Leopard). You know what else is a major animal to see? The elusive Cheetah – though we were not so lucky to see one.

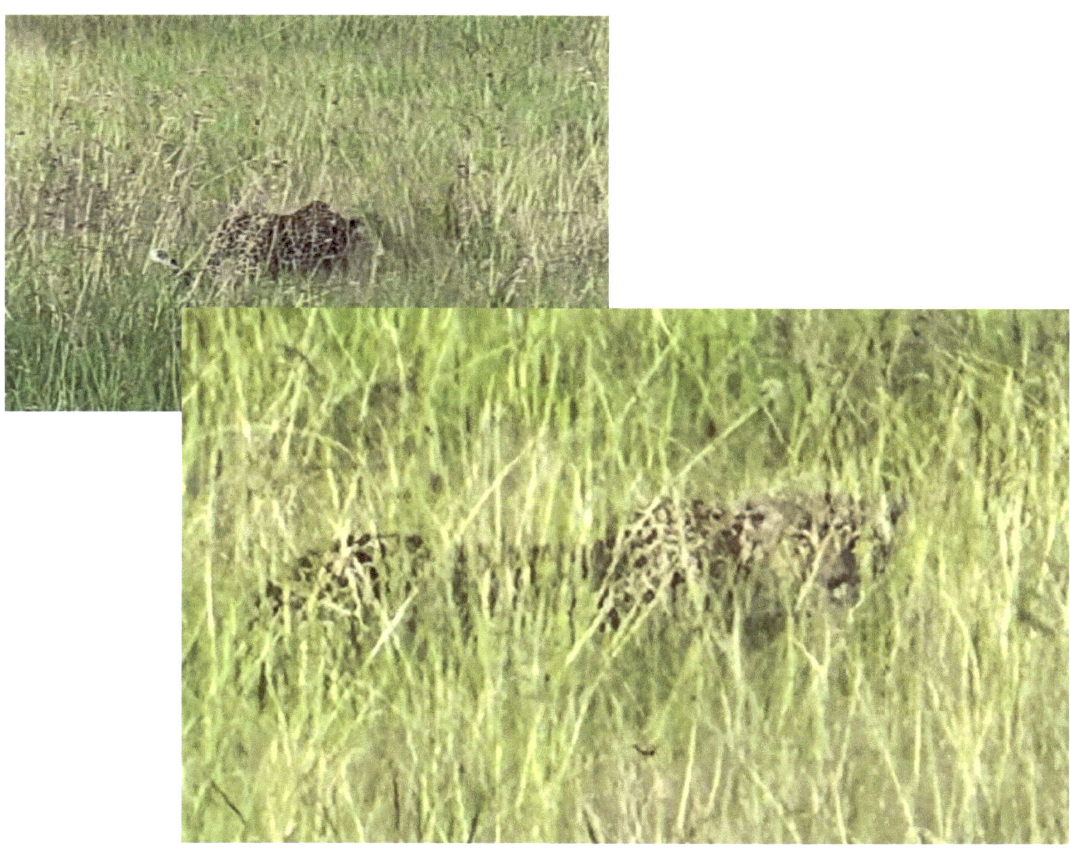

The tips of the leopards' tails are white so the young ones can see their way to follow. Too bad we didn't see any followers. ☺

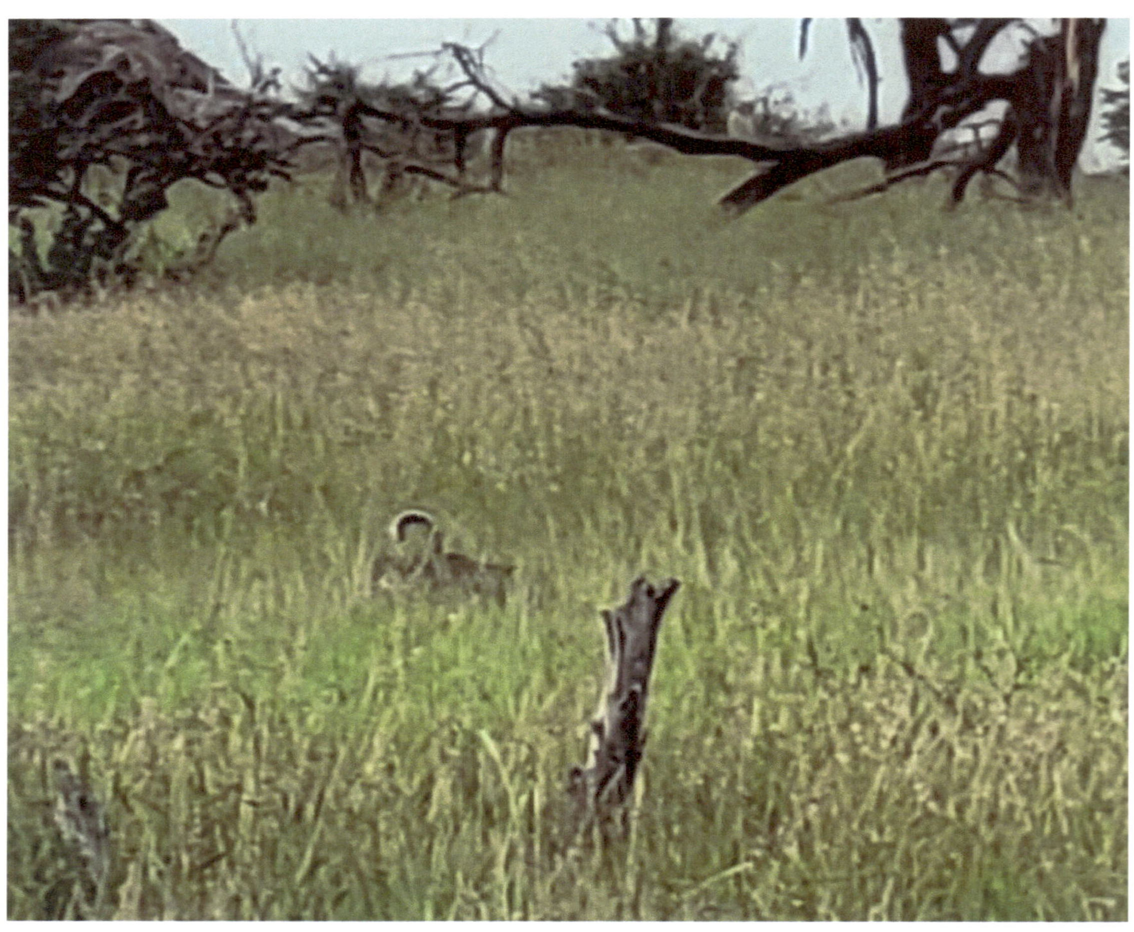

The stuck-jeep-among-lions event and the leopard siting turned an ordinary safari into a wild adventure - at no extra cost, except maybe a tiny bit shorter life! ☺

We arrived at our tent camp on Lion Rock 1.5 hours later, before dark, where there was no rain and a very warm welcome. Whew!

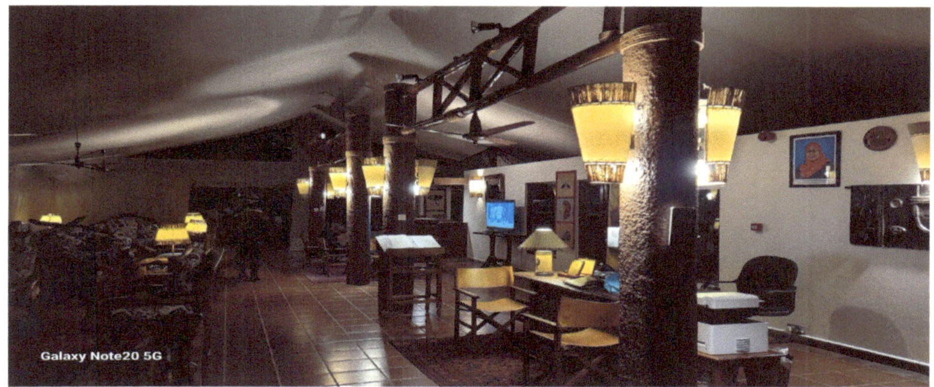

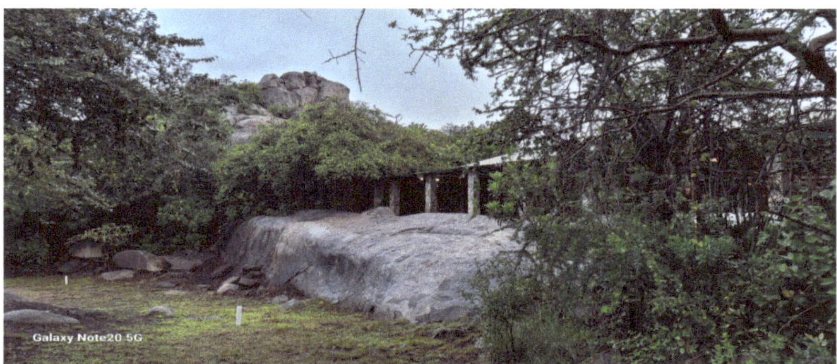

A permanent-tent camp, Mbuzi Mawe Serena (Klipspringer Antelope, "goat (Antelope) stones") Camp at Lion Rock (because the lions home is there!) in central Serengeti, with a gorgeous lobby tent, dining hall, tile floors, and short walls around full bathrooms - glamping - among lions and elephants, both of which visited the camp during the night.

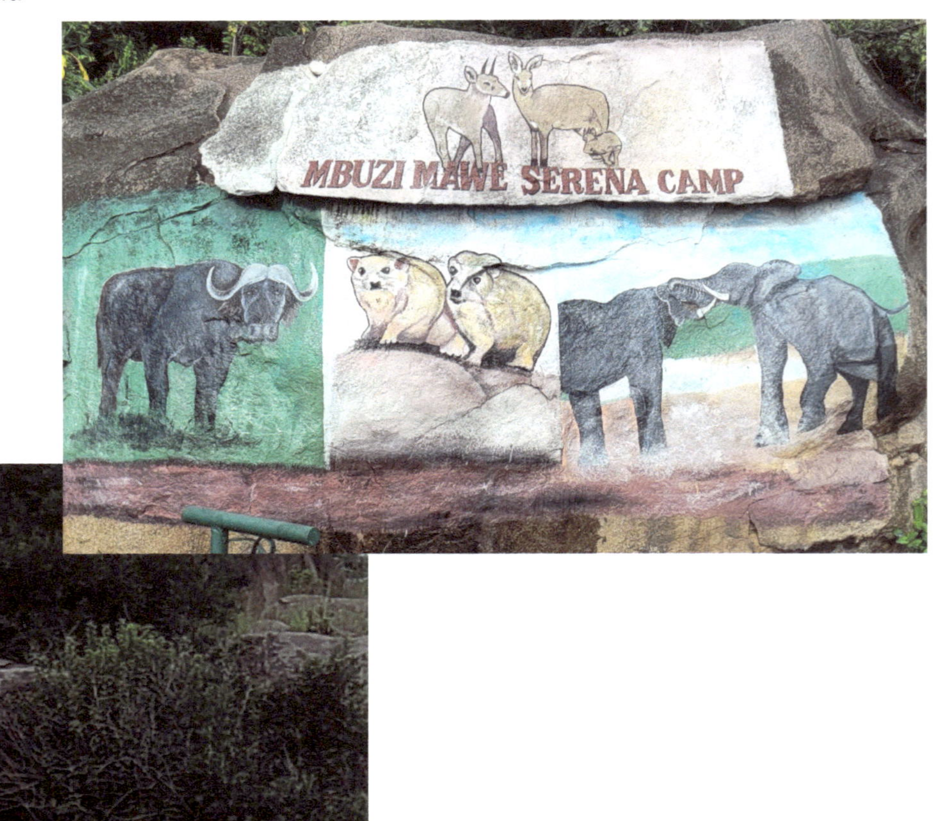

This was our home for 2 nights in the middle of the Serengeti in January, Springtime in East Africa.

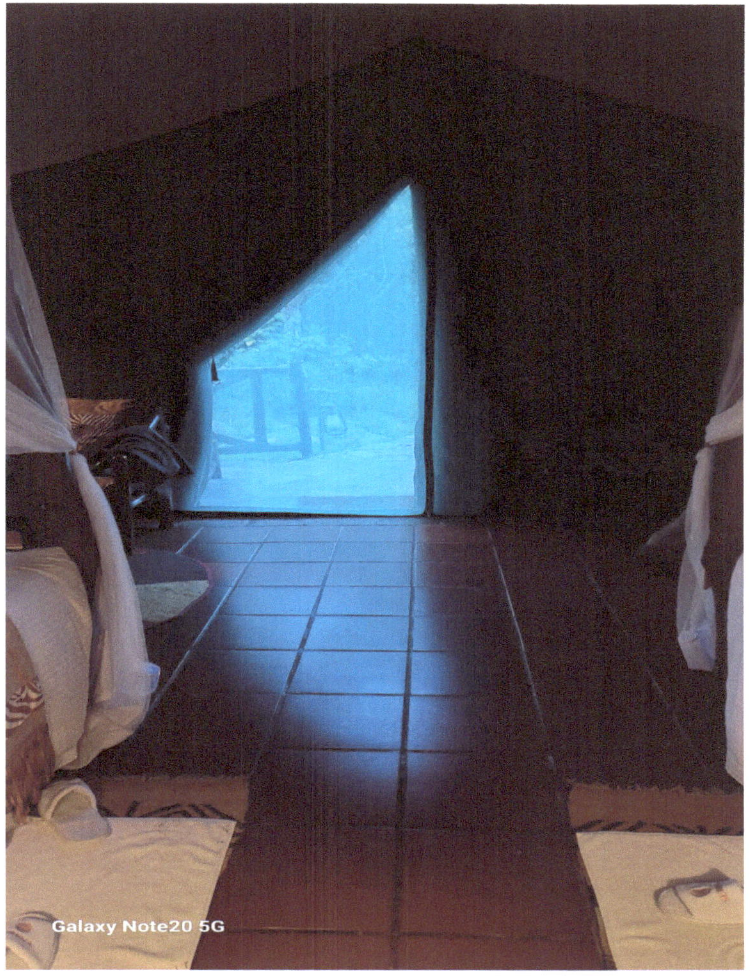

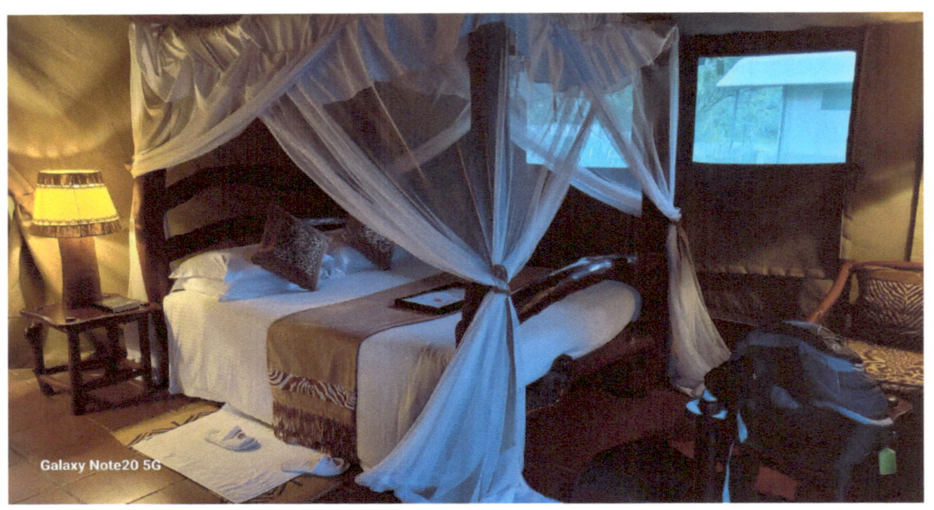

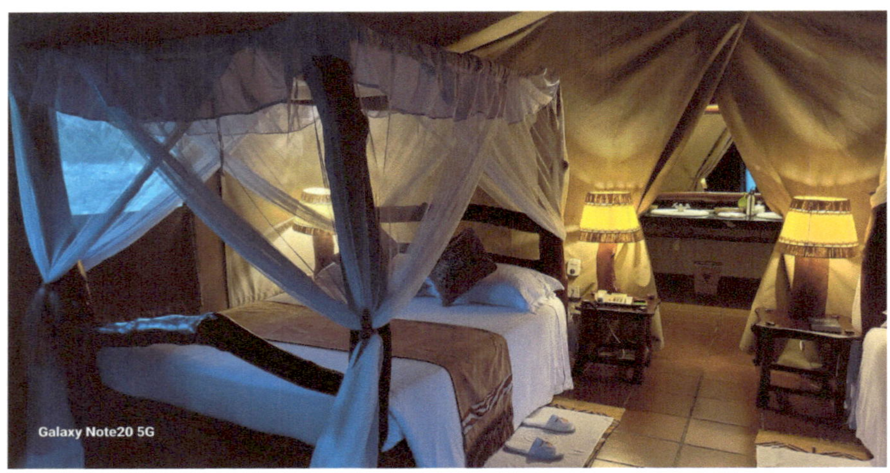

First night, there was a hyena scream and a lion roar that we all heard because it was early after the guards escorted us to our tents after dinner, and not far off from them - after all, the boulder that the camp nestles up to IS called Lion Rock.

The staff said that the hyena kill solved one of the trash-scattering problems at the incinerator. They also said they saw 8 lions after dark in the parking area. I sure hoped we get a promised picture of that (but haven't so far)!

On the 2nd night, we slept through and missed the elephant crashing through the brush outside our tents. zᶻ

The neighboring tent campers didn't miss it though; it happened a few minutes after my journal entries that ended in complete exhaustion at midnight. The couple had passed on attending the day's adventure after the encounter with the lions, and when it came to them instead, they were excited and terrified - they had their own safari adventure without leaving camp!

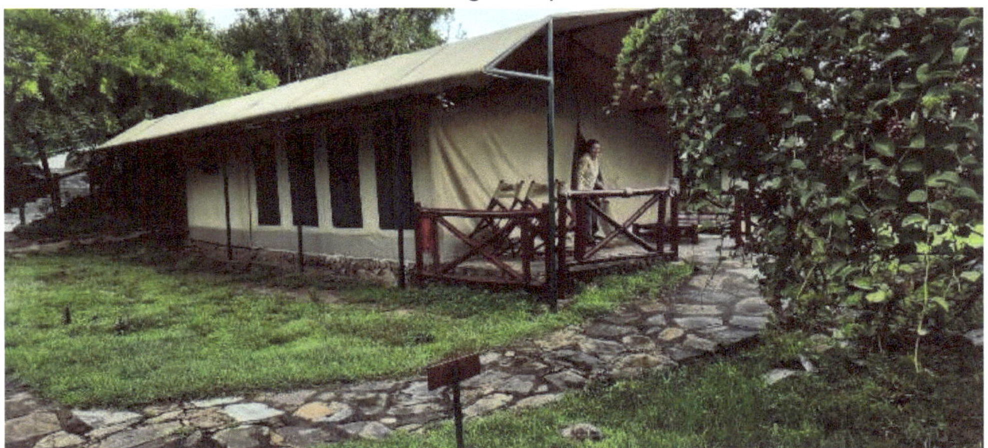

Early, on that last day of safari, we ventured out and got word that a leopard had been sighted in a tree. Because of the distance, our cameras were no match for capturing its glory, but our guide's, Gabriel Kavishe's, camera certainly was, and he sent them to us for our collections.

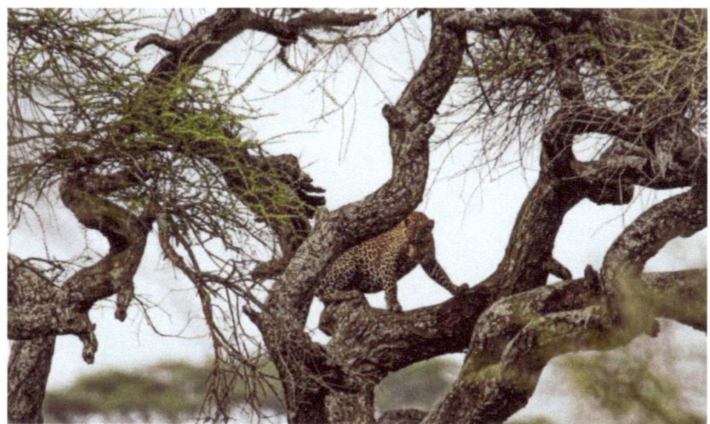

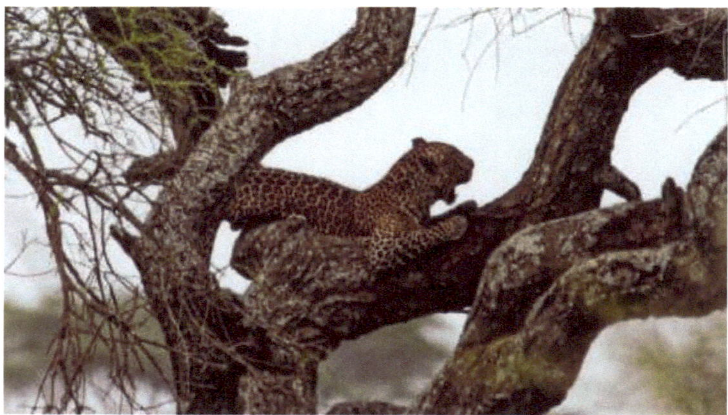

A few more notes:

Maasai Giraffes (vs. Rothschild Giraffes) have varying coat colors.

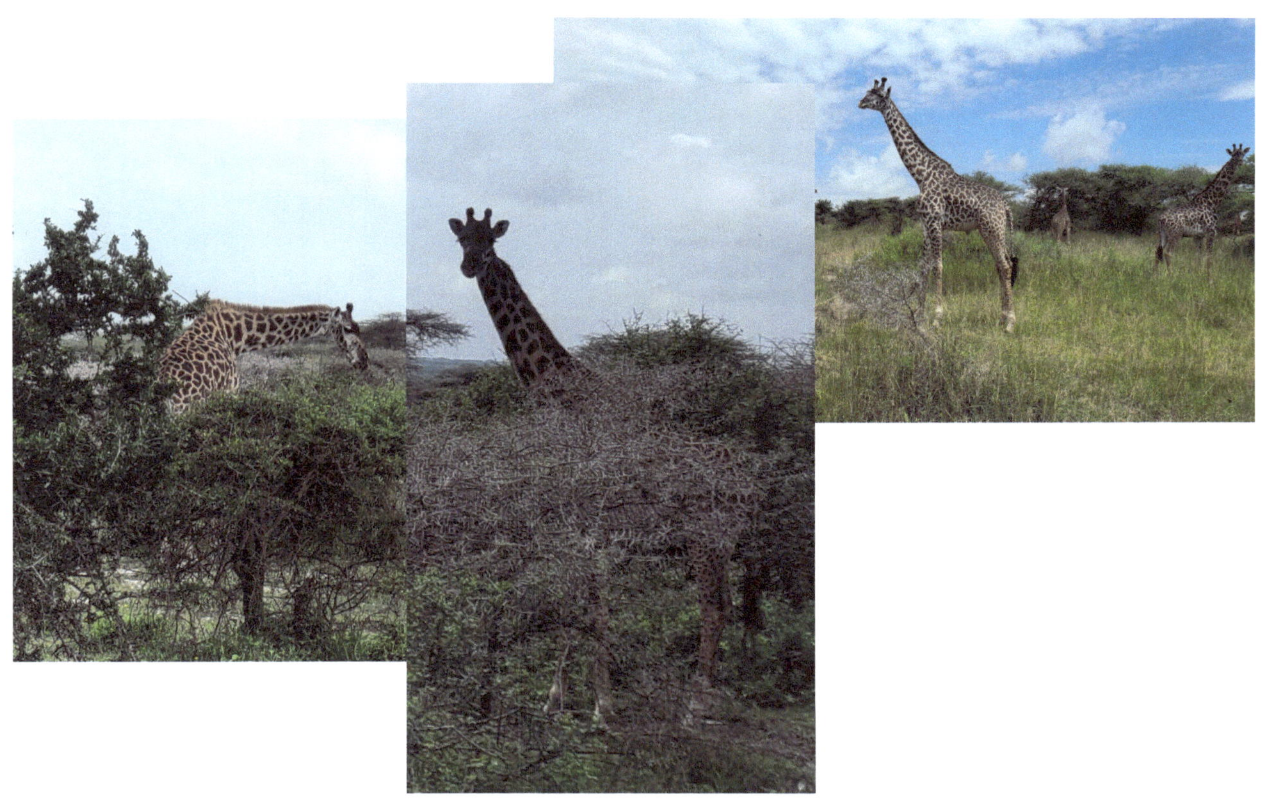

The most vulnerable position a giraffe enjoys is this, taking a drink of water. A lion could take it out. This old boy must have been very careful for a long time.

I was amused by the intrigue this other giraffe experienced about a large rock in the road, "What is this and why is it in the road?" 😀 😵 👻

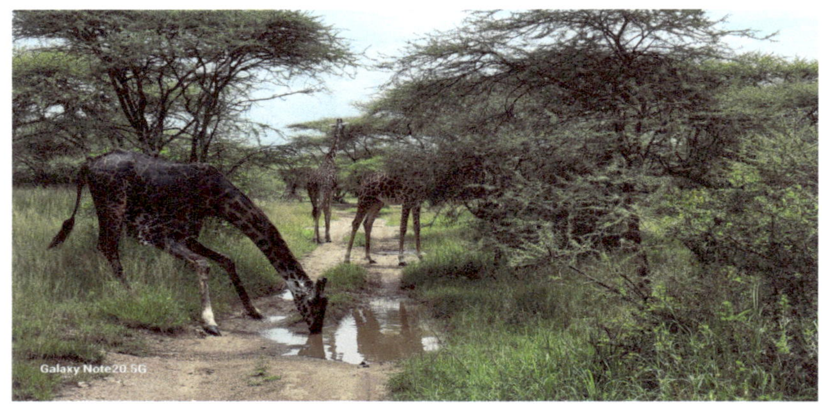

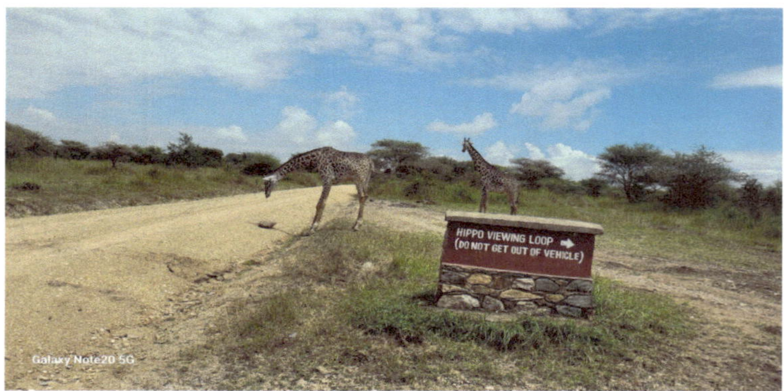

We also came across a lone female lion (possibly, because it's hard to see others that might also be lounging nearby in the midday sun. 🎶

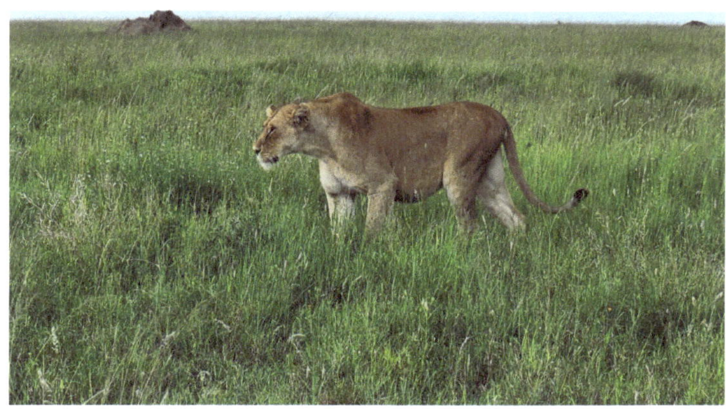

These photos (here and next page) capture a lion pride with nursing cubs resting in the grass. We could barely see 3. Our guide said there could be 6-8. Wow!

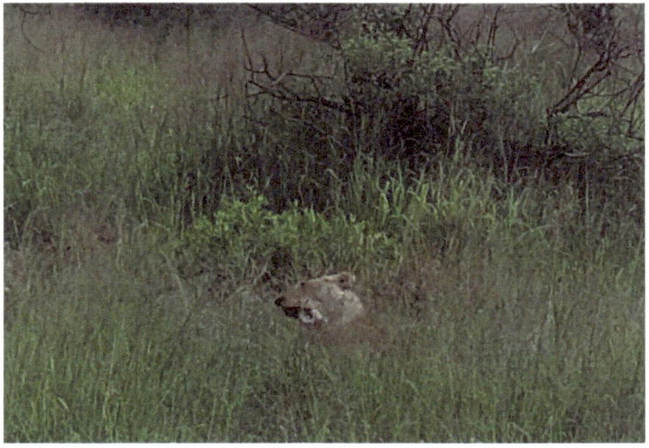

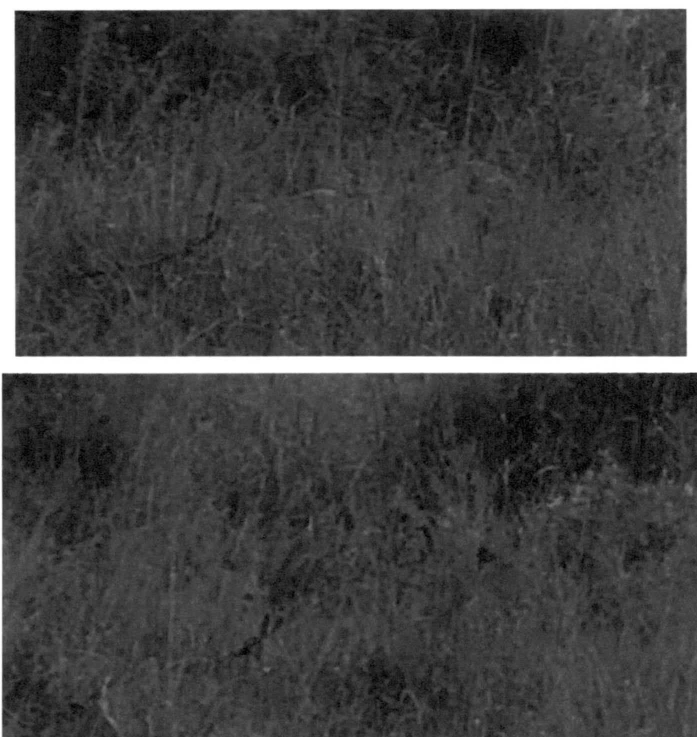

The "Small Five" unique animals, like the Red-billed Buffalo Weaver, are named after the "Big Five"; the next page shows the Leopard Tortoise. There is also a Rhinoceros Beetle. And something small that begins with Elephant and something beginning with Lion. 😁 (I looked them up; they are the Elephant Shrew and the Antlion). For fun, I threw in a picture of the nest of a Buffalo Weaver (we didn't see their red-billed cousin).

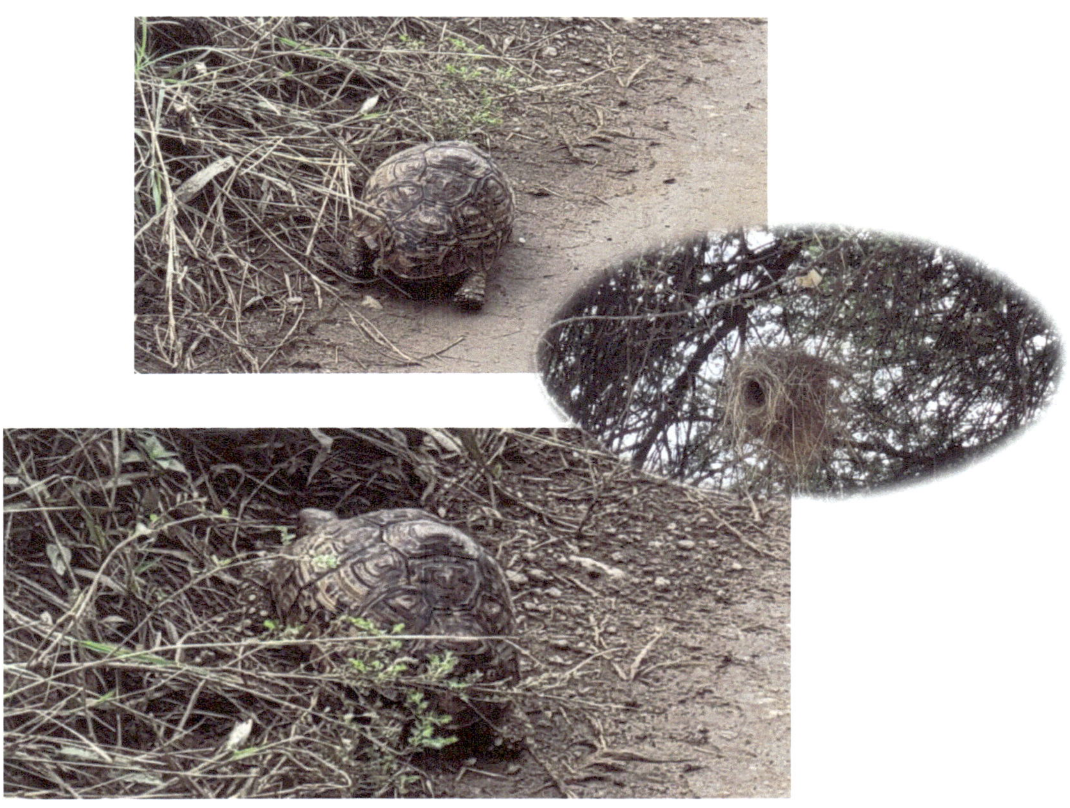

Toughtest dog around ... the Hyena.

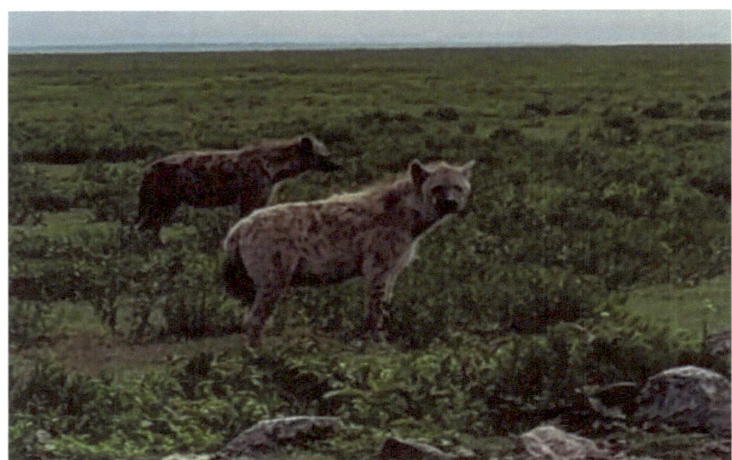

Room to Roam Movement

I assume the Room to Roam initiatives in southern Kenya, on the border with Tanzania that has huge wildlife reserves, allow the wildlife to migrate south and back north, similar to Serengeti migrations for healthy feeding, breeding and mating over changing seasons. The Kitenden Corridor mentioned in the link below is under Kilimanjaro, in the NW section, just above Arusha N. P. in Tanzania.

Our safari guide pointed out the traditional elephant migrations included a corridor to the sea. In particular, he said they migrated to the Saadani N. P. region directly across from the middle of the island of Zanzibar, Tanzania. I hope they restore that corridor over time. He said that the migration is how the elephants historically transferred, through droppings, the coastal palm trees along the corridor to the national parks in the west.

https://www.africanelephantjournal.com/conservancies-woo-landowners-to-mitigate-conflict-with-wildlife/

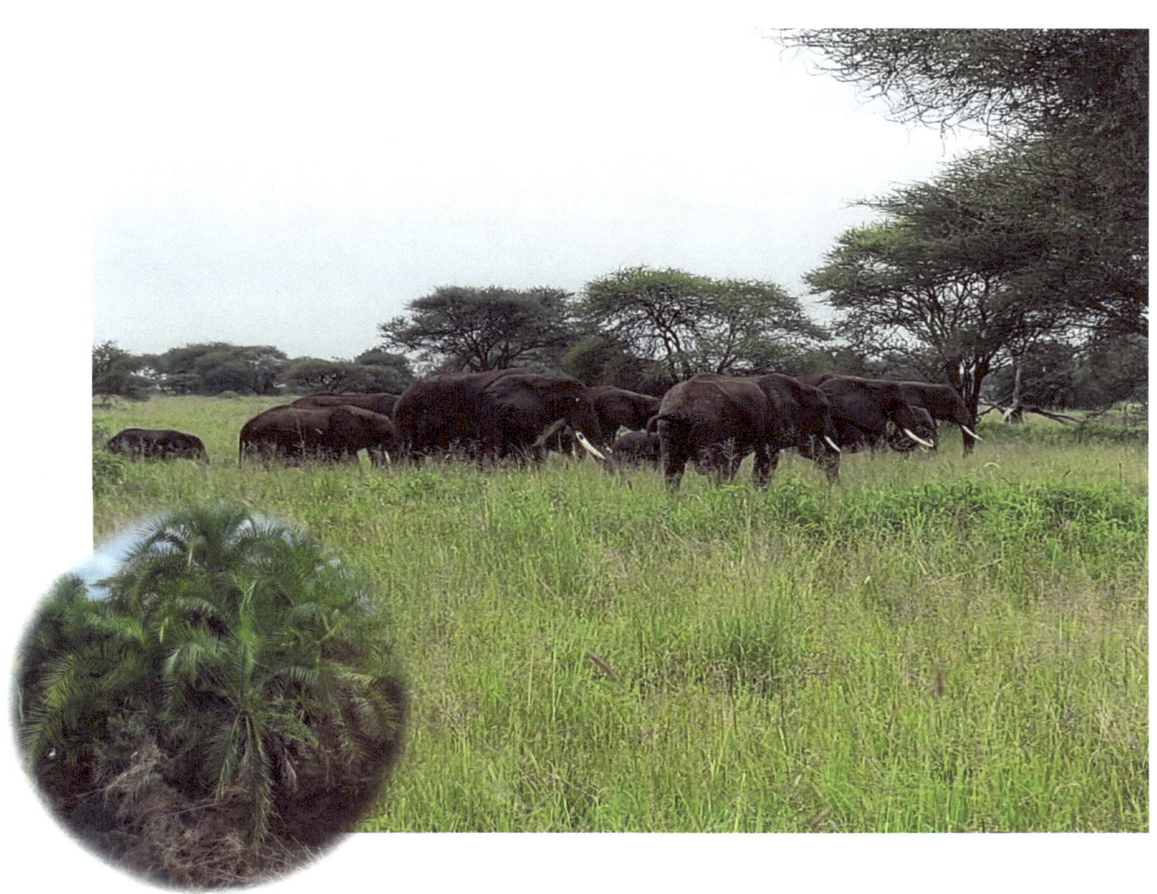

Mpaka tukutane tena, Tanzania. Until we meet again.

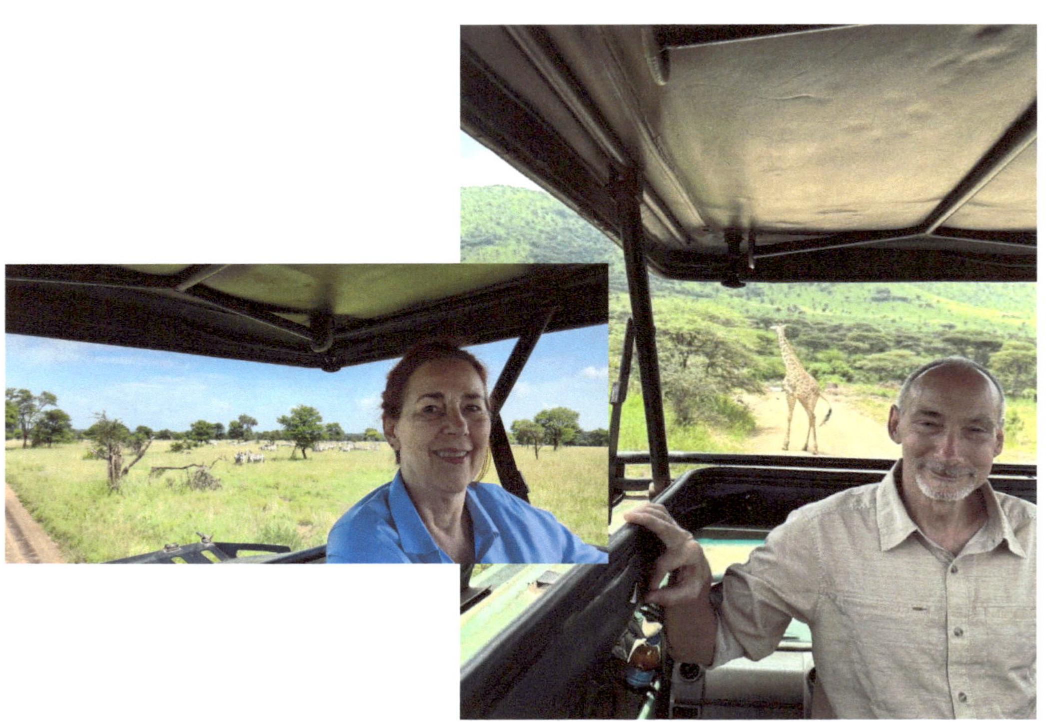

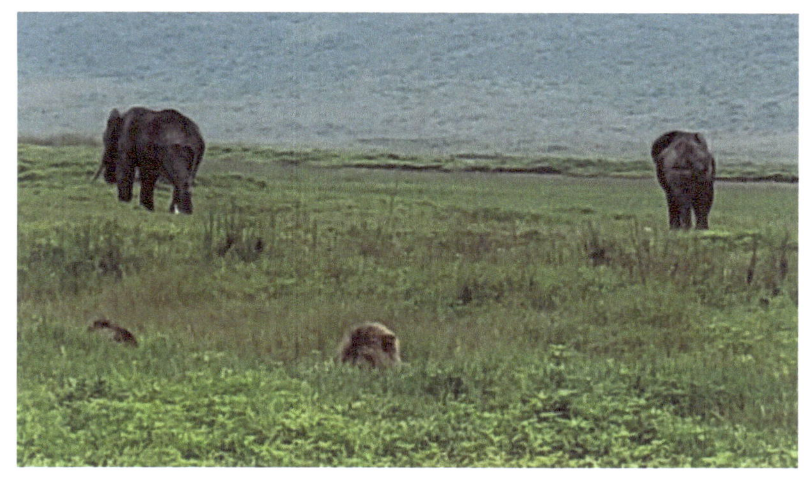

My sincerest gratitude to John Zacher, my heart and soul and fellow traveler, and to Gabriel Kavishe, friend to the animal kingdom, who treated us like family and loving students of nature for nine days one Springtime in Tanzania. His beautiful photography is on Facebook – check out his rhinoceros photo!

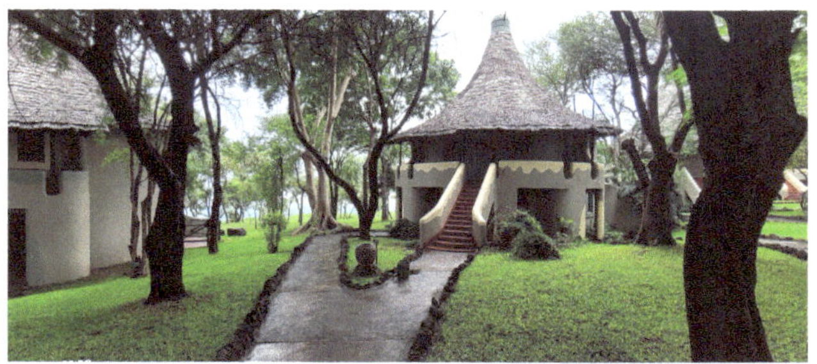

www.ingramcontent.com/pod-product-compliance
Lightning Source LLC
Chambersburg PA
CBHW041600110726

48005CB00002B/236